Job

For Scott,
    May God's peace and
compassion be your
companion on long days
and dark nights.
    David E. Hester

INTERPRETATION
BIBLE STUDIES

Other Interpretation Bible Studies
from Westminster John Knox Press

Genesis
Celia Brewer Marshall

Exodus
James D. Newsome

First and Second Samuel
David C. Hester

Esther and Ruth
Patricia K. Tull

Psalms
Jerome F. D. Creach

Isaiah
Gary W. Light

Jeremiah
Robert R. Laha Jr.

Matthew
Alyce M. McKenzie

Mark
Richard I. Deibert

Luke
Thomas W. Walker

John
Mark A. Matson

Acts
Charles C. Williamson

Romans
Art Ross and Martha M. Stevenson

First Corinthians
Bruce N. Fisk

Second Corinthians
William M. Ramsay

Philippians and Galatians
Stanley P. Saunders

Revelation
William C. Pender

Job

DAVID C. HESTER

WESTMINSTER
JOHN KNOX PRESS
LOUISVILLE · KENTUCKY

Book design by Drew Stevens
Cover design by Pam Poll
Cover illustration by Robert Stratton

First edition
Published by Westminster John Knox Press
Louisville, Kentucky

This book is printed on acid-free paper that meets the American National Standards Institute Z39.48 standard. ∞

PRINTED IN THE UNITED STATES OF AMERICA

05 06 07 08 09 10 11 12 13 14 — 10 9 8 7 6 5 4 3 2 1

Library of Congress Cataloging-in-Publication Data

Hester, David C. (David Charles).
    Job / David Hester. — 1st ed.
        p. cm. — (Interpretation Bible studies)
    Includes bibliographical references.
    ISBN 0-664-22633-7 (alk. paper)
    1. Bible. O.T. Job—Criticism, interpretation, etc. I. Title. II. Series.

BS1415.52.H48 2005
223'.107—dc22   2004056959

Contents

Series Introduction   vi

Introduction to Job   1

UNIT 1   Job 1:1–2:13   7
"There Was a Man Named Job"

UNIT 2   Job 3:1–26   18
"Let There Be Darkness"

UNIT 3   Job 6:1–7:21   28
In the Image of God

UNIT 4   Job 9–10   39
Holding God Accountable

UNIT 5   Job 12:1–14:22   48
Job's Impossible Dream

UNIT 6   Job 19:1–29   58
"I Want to See God"

UNIT 7   Job 29–31   69
Job's Final Appeal

UNIT 8   Job 38:1–40:5   79
Out of the Whirlwind

UNIT 9   Job 40:6–42:6   89
Out of the Whirlwind a Second Time

UNIT 10   Job 42:7–17   99
The Afterword

Bibliography   111
Leader's Guide   113

Series Introduction

The Bible has long been revered for its witness to God's presence and redeeming activity in the world; its message of creation and judgment, love and forgiveness, grace and hope; its memorable characters and stories; its challenges to human life; and its power to shape faith. For generations people have found in the Bible inspiration and instruction, and, for nearly as long, commentators and scholars have assisted students of the Bible. This series, Interpretation Bible Studies (IBS), continues that great heritage of scholarship with a fresh approach to biblical study.

Designed for ease and flexibility of use for either personal or group study, IBS helps readers not only to learn about the history and theology of the Bible, understand the sometimes difficult language of biblical passages, and marvel at the biblical accounts of God's activity in human life, but also to accept the challenge of the Bible's call to discipleship. IBS offers sound guidance for deepening one's knowledge of the Bible and for faithful Christian living in today's world.

IBS was developed out of three primary convictions. First, the Bible is the church's scripture and stands in a unique place of authority in Christian understanding. Second, good scholarship helps readers understand the truths of the Bible and sharpens their perception of God speaking through the Bible. Third, deep knowledge of the Bible bears fruit in one's ethical and spiritual life.

Each IBS volume has ten brief units of key passages from a book of the Bible. By moving through these units, readers capture the sweep of the whole biblical book. Each unit includes study helps, such as maps, photos, definitions of key terms, questions for reflection, and suggestions for resources for further study. In the back of each volume is a Leader's Guide that offers helpful suggestions on how to use IBS.

The Interpretation Bible Studies series grows out of the well-known Interpretation commentaries (Westminster John Knox Press), a series that helps preachers and teachers in their preparation. Although each IBS volume bears a deep kinship to its companion Interpretation commentary, IBS can stand alone. The reader need not be familiar with the Interpretation commentary to benefit from IBS. However, those who want to discover even more about the Bible will benefit by consulting Interpretation commentaries too.

Through the kind of encounter with the Bible encouraged by the Interpretation Bible Studies, the church will continue to discover God speaking afresh in the scriptures.

Introduction to Job

Tucked between Esther and Psalms in Protestant versions of the Bible lies a powerful story of deep faith in tragic times. It is the story of Job and, in a larger sense, it is the story of each of us who has ever tried to make sense of apparently senseless suffering. It is the story of each of us who has ever felt the shattering of relationship with God, with friends and family, and with self. Job arouses readers' passions and challenges well-stroked ideas about the way life is and who God is. It is a book that seizes us, demands our imagination, and refuses to let us go until we have struggled with the same life-shaping questions that haunt its primary character.

Where is God in the worst moments of our emptiness? What are we to do when experience casts doubt on what we have always believed? Where in the world is justice? Is there really any meaning to life? How do I pray to one who has abandoned and betrayed me? These are Job's questions and, truthfully, they are ours as well. They arise from faith to question faith. They are paradoxically questions without firm answers that we must nonetheless ask over and over again. They are questions forced on us by life and death that draw us ever deeper into mystery.

The book of Job is God's word in its most enigmatic form, carried in an ancient tale and a poetic dialogue that raises questions yet shelters answers. What can God be saying to us through the shouting and the silence, the fullness and the emptiness, the joy and the pain of Job's story? What meaning can Job's search for meaning in the midst of piety and pain have for us? How are we to speak of God "truly" in our time and circumstance, as Job did (42:7–8) in his? Job is not comfortable company to be with, even for the limited number of weeks of this study. The valleys of deep darkness (Ps. 23:4) are frightening and lonely places after all. Job's search for God in such a place resonates with our own. For Job the journey through the darkness is ultimately healing. May it be so for us as well.

1

The Wisdom Tradition

The book of Job belongs to a type of writing biblical scholars describe as wisdom literature. It shares this designation with Proverbs, Ecclesiastes, some of the Psalms, and two books in the Apocrypha (which Roman Catholics regard as canonical): the Wisdom of Solomon and the Wisdom of Jesus ben Sirach. These five books constitute the core of Israel's wisdom tradition, but wisdom language and style are found in other places in the Old Testament—for example, in 1 Samuel 30:24–25 and 2 Samuel 5:8. Some have argued that larger units, such as the Joseph Story (Gen. 37, 39–47, 50) and parts of Amos, also belong to the wisdom tradition.

Israel's wisdom literature offers an alternative voice to the louder timbre of the epic narratives of God's wondrous deeds on behalf of Israel's salvation. Missing are the themes of deliverance, wilderness, election, covenant, and exile. Wisdom literature, instead, is focused on coping with life—discerning the rhythm of ordinary existence and learning to live in harmony with it. The good and successful life is one lived in such harmony, and to live wisely is to live in harmony with the Creator, whose mystery is reflected in the very ordering of creation. The way of wisdom, then, is a way of discovery, of attending to human experience, embracing its ambiguities, and testing its truth.

The wisdom tradition is characteristically didactic. Its setting in Israel's life was in institutions responsible for education and instruction, such as the family (or clan) and the royal court, where elders and courtiers passed on to a younger generation their insights gained from reflection on experience in living. The basic tool for this education and the basic literary genre for wisdom teaching was the *mashal*, or proverb. Typically, these wisdom sayings are two lines of verse in parallel structure. For example:

> Whoever is steadfast in righteousness will live,
>   but whoever pursues evil will die.

> (Prov. 11:19)

These sayings "tell it like it is" and often reflect and instill values. By their style, they invite reflection: Is it true to my experience? What about this case? Can anyone really be "steadfast in righteousness"? This basic two-line structure may also develop into longer sayings of three or more lines, but the didactic purpose and grounding in human observation and experience remains. The author of Job even tells us that "Job again took up his *mashal* [NRSV, "discourse"] and said . . ." (27:1), referring to Job's lengthy argument with his three friends. The use of *mashal* here underscores the instructive value of the book as a whole.

Wisdom literature instructs through comparison of things that are similar or things that are dissimilar—or, as in the case of Job, through comparative dialogue. Thematically, creation provides a rich treasure for observation and comparison. For example:

> Go to the ant, you lazybones;
>> consider its ways, and be wise.
> Without having any chief
>> or officer or ruler,
> it prepares its food in summer,
>> and gathers its sustenance in harvest.
>
> (Prov. 6:6–8)

The wise ones observe an order in nature that suggests a similar ordering of human life; the search for wisdom is an effort to discern that order and ways to live in harmony with it. We will see the important role creation themes play in Job, particularly in the speeches of God with which the book climaxes.

Finally, Job takes up a fundamental principle of wisdom literature about how life functions in the world and then debates its truth. Wisdom tradition held that the way of righteousness leads to good life, but that wickedness leads to wrath and punishment (see, for example, Prov. 11:8). It is a principle of just retribution: What one sows, one also reaps; God blesses the righteous with abundant life, but the wicked suffer just punishment. This conviction ran deep in Israel's tradition, particularly in wisdom literature but also in the Deuteronomistic History (recounted in Deuteronomy through 2 Kings) and the prophets. Wisdom tradition viewed this simple equation as an ethical principle inherent in the natural order. For Job, however, the principle of retribution became a critical stumbling block to understanding his own experience. We will have occasion to notice other links between Job and Israel's wisdom tradition along the way, but this brief introduction must suffice for now.

Composition, Authorship, and Date

Every good journey requires a map, and our exploration of Job is no exception. The structure of the book is fairly straightforward:

Prose prologue (chaps. 1–2)
Poetic dialogue between Job and his friends (3–27)
A wisdom poem (28)
Job's closing argument (29–31)
Elihu's speech (32–37)
God's speeches from the whirlwind (38–42:6)
Prose epilogue (42:7–17)

As we shall see, the pieces do not always fit together smoothly. We cannot take up the multitude of issues involved, but they have led scholars to varying conclusions to account for some of the rough junctures between the parts. One obvious question, for example, concerns why the book is bracketed with two prose pieces, while the main body consists of poetry. Or, how are we to account for what appears to be an intrusion by Elihu's speeches between Job's final statements and the appearance of God, which we would expect to come one after another?

Some scholars have concluded that the book's shape reflects its long history of composition in layers: First was an older tale (prologue and epilogue), to which was added poetic dialogue, followed later by the divine speeches, and still later an editorial addition of Elihu's speeches. Other scholars see the book as the work of one author, who made use of a popular folk tale in the prologue and epilogue. I find myself among the latter group. Authorship, in any event, is unknown, and a date for composition depends partly on conclusions about the history of the book's development. Most scholars, however, date the book in the exilic or post-exilic period—that is, between the sixth and fifth centuries BCE. That is important to our task, because events of Israel's life in that period may be relevant for understanding the communal questions to which Job may be responding.

 Want to Know More?

About the Book of Job? See Norman C. Habel, *The Book of Job*, Old Testament Library (Louisville, Ky.: Westminster Press, 1985); J. Gerald Janzen, *Job*, Interpretation (Atlanta: John Knox Press, 1985); Carol A. Newsom, "Job," in *The Women's Bible Commentary*, ed. Carol A. Newsom and Sharon H. Ringe (Louisville, Ky.: Westminster/John Knox Press, 1992); Arnold B. Rhodes, *The Mighty Acts of God*, rev. by W. Eugene March (Louisville, Ky.: Geneva Press, 2000).

About the problem of suffering? See Robert McAfee Brown, *The Bible Speaks to You* (Philadelphia: Westminster Press, 1955), chaps. 11–12; and Shirley Guthrie, *Christian Doctrine*, rev. ed. (Louisville, Ky.: Westminster John Knox Press, 1994), chap. 9.

Studying Job

Forty-two chapters make for a lengthy book, too long for us to be able to discuss each chapter. For that reason, I have selected what I think are critical chapters for understanding the book as a whole. Even at that, your commitment to reading and reflecting on Job will be crucial. The effort will be rewarded, I'm sure. Job has tantalized readers generation after generation; you will likely be caught up in its stormy ebb and flow as well.

It is important that all of you using this Bible study agree to read the chapters assigned by the sessions and reflect on the issues raised in the commentary *out of your own lives.* That means plenty of time needs to be given in each session for discussion and expression of feelings and experiences that may be provoked by your reading. Job is a highly emotional and highly personal book, and that means your group needs to be a safe place where honest opinions and expressions are welcomed and where members are able to care for one another and take the needs of others into account. A study of Job must be as open as the book itself and allow for as much doubt and uncertainty as Job himself experiences.

I come to this writing with my own experience of suffering and the avalanche of feelings and questions that pours from it, and these will undoubtedly become transparent in some of my comments and conclusions. Job is a personal book, and life allows few strangers to the title character's anguish. Job's search throughout is for hope and healing, not by looking past his anger and despair but by facing his dark feelings. We join Job's search; we too long for hope and healing. As for Job, so also for us: This is a journey of faith, possible only by the grace of God and the promise of God's presence. Now we begin.

1

"There Was a Man Named Job"

The story of Job opens with a narrative that introduces us to the principal characters in the book: Job, Job's wife, God, the Satan, and Job's three friends. It is a didactic story, and its peculiar opening (lit., "a man there was in the land of Uz") is reminiscent of the parable of the rich and poor man that Nathan told to David to teach him a lesson (lit., "Two men there were in a certain city," 2 Sam. 12:1). The meaning of Job's name is not clear. Some scholars see it related to a Hebrew word meaning "hated" or "persecuted," images fitting for the Job of the dialogues in chapters 3–27. Other scholars link "Job" to an old Babylonian personal name meaning, "Where is my (divine) father?" Job is mentioned elsewhere in Ezekiel 14:14, 20, and in the apocryphal book the Wisdom of Jesus Ben Sirach (49:9). In Ezekiel, he is mentioned with two

Most scholars now believe the location of "the land of Uz" to be in Edom, the mountains of which can be seen in the distance.

other ancient figures, Noah and Dan'el, all three figures of exemplary righteousness. The Sirach reference recalls the vision of Ezekiel and describes Job as one "who held fast to all the ways of justice." The location of Job's home, the land of Uz, is also unclear. Most scholars now believe it to be in Edom, northwest of Israel and clearly not Israelite territory (see Lam. 4:21).

Whatever the precise meaning of "Job" or location of Uz, the net result for the reader is the sense that we are reading a story that could have started just as well, "Once upon a time, in a land far away, there lived a man named Job." The references to Job in Ezekiel, written in the sixth century BCE, suppose that Job was a legendary figure of righteousness from the ancient past. The author creates for the story a setting in the time of the patriarchs or earlier, putting the story outside the history of Israel and giving it the authority of antiquity. Some have argued that, taken with the closing prose piece in 42:7–17, we have here an ancient and popular legend about a righteous person who suffered great pain and loss, yet in the end is restored to his previous well-being. This view conjectures that the author of Job took an existing popular tale and crafted it to frame the poetic dialogues of chapters 3:1–42:6, the inclusion of which have now complicated the straightforward folktale enormously.

Not only does the enigmatic name of Job and his place of origin provide a "Once upon a time" setting for the story of Job, these features also give it an international flavor or, perhaps better put, a universal setting. Job shares its theme of the innocent suffering of a righteous person with a number of didactic tales found in ancient Egyptian, Akkadian, and Babylonian literature. While similar in some features, none of these works is wholly comparable to Job, and the biblical book certainly does not show any dependence on them. The similarities do suggest, however, that in Job we are dealing with deep and profound issues that have occupied human imagination always and everywhere regarding the meaning of life in the face of suffering and death.

The literary genius of the author of Job is evident right from the beginning. The first two chapters, for example, are structured as five scenes, alternating between earth and heaven. Gerald Janzen sees the structure of this prologue as "emblematic of the structure of the book as a whole" (Janzen, 32). He notes that the pattern visible in chapters 1 and 2—a narrative portion (1:1–5) followed by three scenes in which dialogue dominates (1:6–2:10), followed by a concluding narrative scene (2:11–13)—mirrors the book's overall shape: a narrative prologue (chaps. 1–2), followed by poetic dialogue (3:1–42:6), concluding with a narrative epilogue (42:7–17). In the prologue, the alternating scenes take us from a depiction of Job's full and blessed life—abundant in family and in possessions and scrupulous in practicing his religious duties—to a scene of horror, despair, and misery as Job, now shorn of wealth and family, sits on an ash heap, scraping the inflamed sores that cover his body.

The structure may be outlined like this:

Scene one (1:1–5)—on earth: an introduction to Job, a wealthy, wise, and blameless man

Scene two (1:6–12)—in heaven: God and the Satan create the first test for Job

Scene three (1:13–22)—on earth: the Satan carries out the test; Job remains blameless

Scene four (2:1–7a)—in heaven: God and the Satan devise a second test for Job

Scene five (2:7b–13)—on earth: the Satan carries out the second test; Job remains blameless; Job is joined by three friends, which provides a transition to chapter 3

A careful reading of these scenes reveals a pattern of word and phrase repetition that draws them one to another, intensifying the whole. For example, Job's wealth is described in scene one: a joyful, promising portrayal of an idyllic life. In scene three, however, Job is stripped of his wealth in exactly the reverse order in which it was initially described, so that the pain of his loss builds from stolen oxen and donkeys to the ultimate loss of his children. In response to both tests—the loss of his possessions and the outbreak of terrible sores—Job declares his steadfastness to God with traditional sayings: "Naked I came from my mother's womb, and naked shall I return there; the LORD gave, and the LORD has taken away; blessed be the name of the LORD" (1:21). And in scene five: "Shall we receive the good at the hand of God, and not receive the bad?" (2:10).

At the end of each test as well, the narrator concludes with a statement of Job's innocence: "In all this Job did not sin or charge God with wrongdoing" (1:22) and "In all this Job did not sin with his lips" (2:10). In the two scenes in heaven, the parallels are even stronger. The carefully crafted prologue reveals what the author considers essential for us to know. By seeing what is similar or identical between scenes in the prologue, what is unique stands out as well.

What kind of person is Job? We are told immediately, repeatedly and emphatically, as if to be sure there is no mistake. He is "blameless and upright, one who feared God and turned away from evil" (1:1). These adjectives will figure prominently in the rest of the book, especially the word here translated "blameless" (Heb., *tam*), but the stage is set here. Job is a person of religious, moral, and ethical integrity (Heb., *tumma*; see 2:3, 9). He is faithful in his relationship to God and in following

God's way of life. He loves his neighbor and cares for the poor. He is just, providing fair judgment in cases he is called on to arbitrate. All these virtues are implicit in the phrases "blameless and upright" and "feared God and turned away from evil." Later in the book, in chapter 29, Job will have reason to describe his own behavior—and moral and ethical responsibility—in words that echo this initial judgment of his character. Even now, however, we are right to conclude that Job is a wise and righteous, God-fearing person. Moreover, he is innocent.

God recognizes that Job is blameless and upright. In the scenes in heaven, God celebrates the outstanding character of God's devoted servant, Job. Twice to the Satan, God declares, expansively, "Have you considered my servant, Job? There is no one like him on the earth, a blameless and upright man who fears God and turns away from evil" (1:8; 2:3). God recognizes that Job's remarkable character continues, despite his terrible losses. To the Satan, God says, "He still persists in his integrity [*tumma*], although you incited me against him, to destroy him for no reason" (2:3). Ironically, with this declaration, it is God who seems guilty, not Job, who is unwavering in his loyalty to God even while God "destroy[s] him for no reason."

> A modern version of Job could be written, in which Job heard within ten minutes (*a*) that his house had burned down, (*b*) that his bank had failed, (*c*) that his son had been killed in battle, (*d*) that his daughter had died in an auto accident, and who in the midst of all this (*e*) found that he had polio. He too would ask the question Job asks: "Why has this happened to me?" (Brown 1955, 145)

Above all, the prologue emphasizes that Job is an innocent sufferer, a person of tested faith who holds on to his integrity through unimaginable loss and pain. The whole prologue builds to this conclusion—fundamental to the rest of the book—in which Job protests his innocence despite the friends' insistence that his suffering is irrefutable evidence of his sin or the sin of his children. Job has dutifully taken precaution against the latter case by offering sacrifice routinely for his children (1:5), just in case they should have sinned "in their hearts" (that is, even in their secret thoughts and desires). Job's persistent refusal to let go of his integrity and confess to God and his friends that he has sinned climaxes in his final oath of innocence in chapter 31.

The prologue makes us privy to information that neither Job nor Job's wife nor the friends have—namely, that what Job says about himself is absolutely true and attested by no less a judge than God. The prologue settles a question that plagues the friends throughout the dialogues. They assume as truth that God is just and that God's justice requires righteous behavior to result in success and a good life, whereas a life lived in opposition to God—unmindful of God's ways and devoted to selfish, unethical behavior—leads to emptiness and ruin. In this view, the friends represent a prevalent belief that was common not only in Israel but in other Middle Eastern cultures as well. Job, it must be said, shared this view as well. Nevertheless, the prologue asks us, "consider my servant Job." How is Job's suffering to be accounted for in a world guided by the fundamental association of righteousness with success and a good life? Because Job is declared blameless and upright, his suffering cannot be explained as God's justice, no matter how hard the friends will try. Divine retribution cannot be the explanation here, not if we take seriously Job's innocence.

The alternative raised by the dilemma of innocent suffering is equally difficult. If Job is innocent yet suffering terribly, perhaps it is because God is not just after all but a capricious despot in a world without order or meaning, a world where innocent people suffer without rhyme or reason. Job himself seems to come close to this conclusion in some of his speeches in the chapters that follow our prologue. If we readers are assured of Job's innocence, what does this prologue tell us about God's character and role in Job's undeserved suffering?

A bold, nearly irreverent picture of God appears in scenes two (1:6–12) and four (2:1–6) of this dramatic narrative. Here God, the sovereign king, holds court "on a certain day" (my translation), and the "heavenly beings" (lit., "sons of God") who have been summoned for the occasion present themselves to the king. In the heavenly court, these beings are lesser divine figures who serve as God's courtiers, performing necessary duties assigned by God to carry out God's sovereign rule. Among those who present their reports on this occasion is the Satan. The definite article "the" before "Satan" (Heb., *ha-satan*) indicates a role rather than a personal name. The Satan of our story is not to be confused with the later tradition of a fallen angel by the name of Satan who is God's adversary, the one responsible for devilment in the world. In our story, the Satan is part of God's loyal court; he serves the role of "going to and fro on earth, and . . . walking up and down on it" (1:7; 2:2), presumably to investigate the behavior of human beings. A contemporary analogy might be to see the Satan as a kind of attorney general or prosecutor (see Zech. 3:1).

In the exchange with the Satan, God virtually brags about one outstanding person, Job, whose righteousness is beyond question. "There is no one like him on the earth," God extols. Skeptical to the core, the Satan poses God a challenging question: Does Job worship God "for nothing," that is, freely, for God's own sake, without expecting anything from God in return? Or is Job's piety dependent on the lavish blessings with which God has protectively surrounded (NRSV, "put a fence around") Job and his household? The Satan proposes a test to see what is at the root of Job's exemplary faith: Take away all that protects him and see if he remains a blameless and upright person, "fearing God and turning away from evil." Will Job continue to worship God or will he curse God to God's face (1:11; 2:5)? God agrees to the test and empowers the Satan to strike first Job's family and possessions and, in the second scene, Job himself.

Why God succumbs to the Satan's proposition is ambiguous. Either God is so sure of Job's loyalty that there is no doubt about the outcome of the test or, more likely, God wonders as well about the motivation of Job's piety. Can human beings worship God "for nothing," for the sake of God and nothing else? It is a crucial question and, as Norman Habel thoughtfully suggests, perhaps the Satan is verbalizing God's own latent fears (Habel 1985, 89). In any case, Job is the helpless and hapless victim of a divine test about which he knows nothing. Job's remarkable statements of faith at the end of each test would seem to confirm what God confesses, namely, that God has been incited against Job, "to destroy him for no reason" (2:3). It is not, finally, a comforting picture of God that is portrayed here.

The other figure in the prologue with a speaking part is Job's wife (2:9–10). Overall, women do not play significant roles in the book of Job. Besides Job's wife, the text mentions only the daughters of Job (1:2; 42:13–15), who regularly participate in their brothers' birthday celebrations and who are allotted an inheritance by their father—features unusual in a patriarchal culture. We are not told Job's wife's name; she has no personal identity apart from her relationship to the patriarch. She does have something important to say, however, and the import of her words is strengthened by *when* she speaks: not at the loss of her children and her status as the wife of a well-to-do husband who provided at least a modicum of security, but only later, when loathsome sores cover her husband from head to toe. As Job sits among the ashes, scraping his sores, his wife (we can imagine) fairly shouts at him, "Do you still persist in [Heb., "seize hold of"] your integrity? Curse God, and die." Her outburst—whether born of despair or sympathy for her husband, who seems as good as dead— is composed of a phrase that recalls God's evaluation of Job at the end of the first test ("he still persists in his integrity," 2:3) and a phrase that reflects the Satan's prediction of Job's response to his suffering ("he will curse you to your face," 1:11; 2:5).

For this advice, Job's wife has received harsh treatment at the hands of commentators over the centuries, including Augustine and Calvin, who saw her as the Satan's ally. Job's response to her comment is disparagement, describing her speech as that of a fool. Yet one wonders, as some scholars suggest, whether her words might not capture something of Job's own hidden thoughts. Just as the Satan gives voice to God's doubts about Job's motives for worship, perhaps Job's wife reflects Job's own latent feelings and arising doubts.

Carol Newsom calls attention to the two sides of integrity (Newsom 1996, 356). On the one hand, integrity refers to fulfillment of commitments, in this case the traditional duties and service of an "upright" worshiper of God, but integrity also suggests giving credence to one's experience. For Job, there is a growing tension between these two sides of integrity, as Job's experience of suffering questions the truthfulness of the traditional explanation that links sin and suffering. Thus, Job's wife serves an important role in the narrative, providing readers with insight into an internal struggle developing in Job. Job does not curse God, but he will curse the day of his birth (chap. 3) and speak longingly of death for himself. Newsom concludes thoughtfully; "Job's wife is the prototypical woman on the margin, whose iconoclastic words provoke defensive condemnation but whose insight serves as an irritant that undermines old complacencies" (Newsom 1992, 132).

> Do people suffer in exact proportion to their sinning? The book of Job says an emphatic "No!" And so does Jesus (John 9:1–3). You cannot necessarily measure a person's sin by the suffering endured. (Rhodes, 206)

Job, the prologue is clear, does not deserve the suffering that he receives at the hand of God. No refuge is taken in secondary causes: God is responsible for the suffering of a blameless person of faith. Nor in these chapters does Job ever raise the question of why he is suffering. He does not know what the reader knows; he knows nothing of the debate between God and the Satan. The book of Job reserves for chapter 3 and later the anguished cry of "Why?" that we know so well when suffering comes. The prologue chooses to focus on another question: How does a person of deep faith and close relationship with God respond to undeserved suffering? Initially, Job turns to two wisdom sayings drawn from the tradition, but this is just the beginning of the story. Job's response grows more complex as his suffering intensifies and undeniable feelings and troubling questions fester from his wounds.

The prologue ends with Job sitting in grief and silence, seeking comfort in the ironic effort to ease the pain of his sores by digging at them with a piece of broken pottery. There is no relief in sight, no happy ending apparent. How then is a person of faith to live this way? What happens to one's relationship to God and to others and to oneself? What becomes of meaning in life? Where is God in our suffering? The prologue invites us to imagine that all these questions swirl in Job's ravaged head during those seven silent days and nights sitting on the ash heap. They are questions that carry us beyond chapters 1–2 into the rest of the book, until an end to the suffering finally comes.

Job 2:11–13 provides us with a final scene that firmly connects these opening chapters with the rest of the book. The setting shifts suddenly to focus on three of Job's friends: Eliphaz, Bildad, and Zophar. As in the case of Job and Uz, it is unclear where these three friends come from but, once again, the homes are located outside Israel. We are told very little about the friends, though they will reveal much of their thought in the cycle of speeches that constitute chapters 3–27. How they heard of Job's suffering we are not told, but, importantly, we are told they meet together to go to "console and comfort" Job. They go intending to relieve Job's suffering. Ironically, they will, instead, intensify it.

We are told of their horror at seeing their friend, so disfigured by his suffering that they did not recognize him. That is an experience some of us know painfully well. We too have gone to homes or to hospitals to visit friends whom we may not have seen for some time, only to find them so changed by debilitating disease and constant pain that we hardly recognize them. Like Job's friends, we can be moved to tears by what we see—empathetic tears, to be sure, but tears for our sorrow as well. Consolation requires the kind of empathetic solidarity the friends show toward Job at the beginning of their time together.

The friends, we may imagine, last visited Job in his fine house, surrounded by his loving family. Now they sit with him in ashes, bereft of his children, a homeless and disgusting figure. One wonders what they could possibly say or do to comfort him. A ministry of presence is a good beginning, but silence must give way in time to speech. Then what will they say to Job? We will have to wait to hear. For now, the story finds a resting place on an open wound: "No one spoke a word to him, for they saw that his suffering was very great" (2:13).

Remarkable as the artistry of the Job writer is in these two chapters, as well as throughout the book, what draws us into the story finally is the way these several scenes touch our experience. All of us have known suffering and loss, some more radical and pervasive than others. Suffering and loss are a part of the human condition, yet they come to us as thieves in the night to steal the modest security and sense of well-being we create for ourselves. Broken relationships, isolation, a desperate longing for peace, imbalance, loss of focus, fear, anger, tears, and grief—these conditions accompany suffering and loss, and we know them all. Job's loss is extreme, to be sure. His means of making a living is gone, his standing in the community altered, and, above all, his heart is torn like his clothing with the death of his children and extended family. Worse, his pain and anguish become visible in the ugly, repulsive sores that cover his body. Extreme, yes; yet somehow we have a part in it. We can imagine Job's suffering because we know our own. Our experience is not "just like" Job's.

 Want to Know More?

About Job 1–2? See J. Gerald Janzen, *Job*, Interpretation (Atlanta: John Knox Press, 1985), 31–34.

About the Satan? See Arnold B. Rhodes, *The Mighty Acts of God*, rev. by W. Eugene March (Louisville, Ky.: Geneva Press, 2000), 204; and Carol A. Newsom, "Job," in *The Women's Bible Commentary*, ed. Carol A. Newsom and Sharon H. Ringe (Louisville, Ky.: Westminster/John Knox Press, 1992), 130–31.

No one can dare to claim to know exactly what another's suffering is like. Yet our experience allows us to identify with Job and calls us to listen to his story in solidarity with him.

Job's suffering is not, however, about suffering in general. It is about the suffering of a person of deep religious conviction. We human beings must make sense of our experiences; they must mean something in the context of our lives and the order we find in life generally. For Job, as for us, suffering must make sense in some fashion within the framework of faith that constitutes Job's way of understanding how life is. If it cannot, then the truth of Job's perspective must be rethought and altered or abandoned.

Job's tradition offers multiple reasons to account for suffering, as we shall see in the arguments of the friends. For Job, the reason for his suffering is the mysterious providence of God, who "gives and takes away" and from whom we receive "good and bad." How adequate an answer is that to the devastation of a "blameless and upright" person?

Perhaps it is less an answer than a shout of protest into an overwhelming wind. Job's suffering cannot be accounted for as "natural"—as in, for example, the death of an elderly parent—nor can it be accounted for by Job's sin or self-destructive behavior, as the resounding assurance of his innocence and admirable conduct in the prologue make clear. Job's suffering is undeserved by any account. It is purposeless, as even God declares.

We face the same challenge that Job faces: How do we make sense of radical suffering in the light of our deepest convictions about who God is and how God is related to us, to the events of our lives, and, ultimately, to all creation? If we cannot make sense of it, how do we live faithfully with God, with friends, and with ourselves? The prologue drags us into questions like these, some of which we would rather avoid. As persons of faith in a broken world of radical suffering, however, we have a vested interest in Job's story. We dare not look away.

The prologue asks another question of us as well, one that will also trouble the rest of the book. The Satan's question to God, about which God seems genuinely concerned—"Does Job fear God for nothing?"—is a question for us too. The Satan implies that Job's worship of God is the result of God's protective hedge being placed around Job, his family, and his way of life. He worships, the Satan suggests, to put it crudely, because there is something in it for him. Worship is Job's "hedge" against losing the life he enjoys. The only way to test the truth of the Satan's charge and to assuage God's doubts is to take the hedge away from Job and see whether reverence turns to betrayal.

The question calls for some soul searching. Why do we worship God? Do we worship God for God's sake, or to secure ourselves in a threatening world? Is it what God has done or may do for us that makes God worthy of worship? Is our worship, even in ways of which we may be unaware, manipulative of God? Do we worship God to get what we want or think we need? Can you worship God in those times when you may feel abandoned or even betrayed by God? Where is the place where your relationship with God finally breaks, if you can imagine such a place? How do you "sing the LORD's song" (Ps. 137) in such a foreign place? In the prologue, Job proves himself steadfast in his worship, but that is not the end of the story. We have more to hear, and the question about our reason for reverence looms.

Chapter 1 began with fanfare, celebrating a blameless and upright servant of God who enjoyed a full and peaceful life. The close of chapter 2, however, is pathetic. Peace is replaced with horrified silence and the dark shades of depression; joy has turned to mourning. Job's comforters are speechless, waiting for Job to break his lonely vigil. Seven days and seven nights they have sat like this, a still photo waiting for resolution. In the long silence, the author invites us to imagine what is going on in Job's heart and mind. What questions throb there, what doubts? What angry impulses surge? Seven days represents a standard time for mourning rites, but what will Job do after that? How is life to go on for him?

? Questions for Reflection

1. Job is described as a man of integrity, one who is "blameless and upright," "who fears God and turns away from evil." What does having integrity mean to you? Can you think of some modern examples of people whom you would call blameless and upright? Who are they, and what are they like?
2. We hear people say (and maybe we say it ourselves) that people get what they deserve. What do they (we) mean by that?
3. Why do we worship God? What would it mean to worship God "for nothing"?
4. Job's friends heard of his suffering and came to console and comfort him. When they saw him they were shocked and moved to tears, and they sat with him in silence. Have you had experiences like this? Talk about them carefully with each other.

2 Job 3:1–26

"Let There Be Darkness"

The silence has been deafening. For seven days and nights, Job and his three friends have sat in speechless suffering. What a contrast with the immediate declaration of faith (1:21) that Job fairly shouted in the face of disaster when God's name was blessed in the face of bitter loss! Even the more ambiguous rhetorical question with which Job counters his wife's humane urging that he "curse God and die" affirms trust in the providence of God: "Shall we receive the good at the hand of God, and not receive the bad?" (2:10) What, we wonder, has been going on in Job's mind during this long lapse in dialogue or action of any kind? We who can barely stand a minute of silence in the company of others can only imagine long days and nights in solitary contemplation. Silence can be healing and revitalizing. There is a monastery not far from where I live where the rule of the day is silence for the brothers who live there, apart from the hours of prayer or to welcome guests. People from the area often retreat to this sacred place of peace precisely for the renewal that meditating in silence over several days affords. Was this the kind of silence Job kept, one searching for healing and restoration?

Or was Job's silence of a different order, a silence of suffering, a forced silence because there are no words to touch the depth and breadth of pain, a silence of utter loneliness that blocks out even well-meaning friends who awkwardly offer consolation and comfort? Perhaps Job is at a loss for words, robbed of self-expression by overwhelming agony that distances oneself from self, from others, and even, perhaps, from God. Suffering in silence is an experience we know when suffering is soul deep, when the mind swirls and twists in search of thoughts to speak to oneself that can somehow reconstruct a life that once seemed anchored but now careens madly off course toward chaos. Yet thoughts remain garbled, tumbling over each other in search of sense, confusion and nonsense ever pressing downward toward an enveloping darkness. Perhaps Job's silence is like this, a silence of shock and bewilderment, a silence of confusion, a silence of protest against the unhinging of the world as we have known it, a silence of doubt and fear that our deepest beliefs cannot withstand the scrutiny of our suffering.

Suffering cannot bear the silence indefinitely. Grief must find its voice or the heart will burst. Psychologists have taught us that good grief must find expression for feelings of loss, fear, and emptiness if mourning is to be a healing process, as it should be. Suffering must find its voice to be endured and, hopefully, resisted. The flood of thoughts, questions, and doubts dammed up behind the clinched teeth of silence burst through in shouts, sobs, and tears. How long this process takes to move from silence to voice not surprisingly varies from person to person. For Job, the poet-author tells us, it took seven days and seven nights. Seven is a symbolic number and suggests here a completed period of silence, that is, "when the right time came." "After this Job opened his mouth and cursed the day of his birth" (3:1).

Job's silence is broken with a soliloquy that opens to us his deepest thoughts. Apart from two brief wisdom sayings in chapters 1–2, we have not heard from Job until now, making the contrast between Job's declarations there and here all the more dramatic. He shatters silence with a curse. Has the Satan won after all, since he said that once God's protection was removed, Job would curse God to his face? Job's wife advised him to "curse God and die," and Job rebuffed her, yet now he begins his self-disclosure with a curse. In point of fact, Job does not here curse God—not exactly. He splits a hair and curses, rather, the day of his birth, a day God created. Still, his words are powerful and, if taken seriously, intended to affect the whole of creation. In Job's world, cursing is not incidental, as it is in ours. It is deadly serious business because the curse is assumed to become effective, releasing real powers whose role it is to bring the curse to fruition. Curses inaugurate destruction, the very opposite of a blessing's promise of well-being (see Deut. 28:1–46).

Job curses the day of his birth (3:3a, 4–5) and the night of his conception (3:3b, 6–9), and would thereby alter that day on the calendar forever:

Let the day perish [lit., "be destroyed"] in which I was born,
and the night that said,
"A man-child is conceived."

(3:3)

Never again would that day be a day of joy and celebration, but a sunless day of deep gloom, as if a funeral pall had been cast over it perpetually.

That night—let thick darkness seize it!
let it not rejoice among the days of the year;
let it not come into the number of the months.

(3:6)

Scholars have seen in Job's curses a reversal of the creation story in Genesis 1–2. The clearest example of that may be verse 4, in which Job's words, "As for that day, let it be darkness!" (my translation), reverse God's first words of creation, "Let there be light!" Indeed, in the Genesis account, light dominates everything, as God brings what was created into light. In Job's undoing of creation, darkness dominates, with four different Hebrew words for it in these verses. "In the beginning," the Genesis story says, "the earth was a formless void," a chaos of unrestrained forces. Leviathan, the giant and fierce sea creature, is a symbol of that chaos (see Ps. 74:12–17; Job 40:25), and Job would "stir up" this creature to return the day of his birth to a time before creation. Instead of being fruitful and multiplying, the human beings of Job's imagination are impotent, the night barren, with no joyful cry of sexual intimacy (3:7). As Roland Murphy observes, "Paradoxically, night itself is to be enveloped in darkness, as the evening stars stop shining and dawn fails to appear" (Murphy 1999, 19).

Birthdays are ordinarily for remembering, a celebration of existence. Job's day is to be forgotten, since existence is nothing to celebrate, so darkened as it is by pain, grief, and senselessness. Whatever good times there may have been can provide no comfort for Job now. Once birthdays were celebrated with great parties by Job's family (1:4). Now the night in which he was conceived is cursed,

because it did not shut the doors of my mother's womb,
and hide misery from me.

(3:10; my translation)

Curses make up less than half this chapter, however. With verse 11, Job begins a long lament or complaint, punctuated with five "why" questions (vv. 11, 12, 16, 20, and implicitly 23). We are familiar with laments from the Psalms, where that form dominates the types of hymns included in the Psalter (see Ps. 13; 32). Lament psalms ordinarily appeal to God for help, because the worshiper is suffering oppression or is surrounded by enemies or because, for one reason or another, relationship with God has been broken. The complaint usually moves from a cry for help, to a description of the situation, to a declaration of the worshiper's trust in God (see Ps. 13:3–6). But that is not the case with Job's complaint. He does not explicitly appeal to God for help, and the complaint shows no evidence of confidence or trust in God. Indeed, his words do not ask for help at all, and God is barely mentioned. Rather, Job continues the probing self-examination of one who finds the possibility of death more attractive than life. "Why did I not die at birth?" he asks. But it is a wish more than a question. "Why was I not buried like a stillborn child?" never even seeing the light of day. If it were just for misery that I was born, Job suggests, then it would be better never to have lived at all.

It is natural for human beings to cling to life, but, in a monumental reversal of human nature, Job longs for death. In his fantasy, Job extols the virtues of Sheol, the place of the dead in Hebrew thought. Ordinarily, Sheol is not described as an attractive place to go. It is a place of gloom, a godforsaken place where the dead are not remembered by God or touched by God's love (Ps. 88:3–5, 10–12; Job 10:21–22). Compared with his present life, Job sees even nonlife in the place of the dead more appealing. It is a place of quiet and sleep. It is a place where social distinctions are leveled and where those who are oppressed in life are finally free from their taskmasters. Had he died at birth or even in the womb he would have been more fortunate, Job seems to think, than kings and princes, who, like himself, gather wealth and prestige in life only to lose it to the grave. What attracts Job to the grave is the promise of quiet and rest and freedom from his suffering. Death is a refuge for Job from an unbearable life:

> For my sighing comes as my bread,
>> and my roarings are poured out like water.
> For the fear I feared has happened to me,
>> and what I dreaded has come to me.
> I have no ease, no quiet, no rest,
>> but turmoil came.

> (3:24–26; my translation)

Suffering has taken over Job's life; it is with him morning and night. It is the one staple of his life, his bread and water emptied of any nourishment. More intense than any physical pain, dread and fear control him. For this man—once so sure of himself because meaning and purpose in life seemed clear and his relationship with God was not in doubt—life has become confusion, dread, and alienation. These themes continue through the book, but collected here they create an intense portrait of a human life pushed to the brink by life-emptying suffering. The story's prologue told us of Job's terrible losses, led us to imagine ourselves faced with the death of our children, vividly compelled us to look at Job's oozing sores, while affirming his steadfast trust in God. Yet words of assurance drawn from his tradition can no longer bear the weight of Job's suffering. All that grounded Job seems pounded into the dust and ashes in which he sits. A wise man once confident of life now eats sighing for bread and drinks his cries of pain like water. Life, once well ordered and directed, now is terrifying, and Job is filled with dread. The loss of life he mourns is not only that of his family but his own life also. Now he wishes he had never been born, if it was only for the purpose of unrelenting suffering that he saw the light of day.

Job seems in this chapter to edge toward suicide. He longs for death and sees it as his only hope for freedom from his torment. In truth, he longs for life—but breathing is not enough for life; life must be worth living. It must offer more than daily fear and dread. There must be purpose to life. There must be what we now call "quality of life." That characteristic is hard to quantify and different for each person, but we recognize it when we don't have it. And we wonder about what kind of life there must be for friends or family members who bear tragedy in their body or their mind.

Extended life, which science seems to keep promising to us these days, raises the question of quality of life more sharply still. Where life is unbearable, death may seem preferable. Increasing numbers of assisted suicides attest to tragic moments like these. So also do the staggering numbers of suicides and suicide attempts recorded annually among young people. A 1997 survey of high school students, for example, reported that one in five young people had seriously considered suicide during the preceding year, and most of them had drawn up a suicide plan (Jamison, 22). Suicide is the second leading cause of death among teens and the third among people under thirty-five. Lest we forget, these statistics are someone's children, someone's husband or wife, father or mother—all people who sought relief in death from the desperate pain of prolonged illness or from the daily internal agony of mental disease.

Job is not a suicide, however, nor need we see him as severely depressed. He clings to life in his outcry against its emptiness, constant turmoil, and misery. The dread and fear with which he lives accompanies any and all of us for shorter or longer moments in our lives. Death, disease, and loss are unavoidable powers in our lives, twisting us off center. Dread and fear overtake us in our vulnerability. Perhaps we have been wrong, we think; perhaps life counts for little or nothing. Perhaps emptiness is all there is. Suffering makes us entertain the possibility that this is true. Suffering makes us fear that nothing will change, that the pain we feel now will be our daily bread, as it was for Job: no ease, no quiet, no rest—only turmoil. We dread and fear a life like that, overwhelmed by worry and anxiety. No purpose. No meaning. No sense of direction. We might have said it that way. What kind of life is that? It is a living death. We have all known moments of despair like that. For many in our society and around the globe, it is routine. Some are terminally ill children with their parents, terminally impoverished families, victims of AIDS, refugees living in makeshift shelters, battered women, and sensitive men, women, and children who care for them all—a large company of persons for whom life is bathed in suffering.

> Why me? Why anyone? Why does God . . . ? Why doesn't God . . . ? What am I to do? How can I endure? What's next? What does it all mean? Questions are more numerous than answers. Many answers raise new questions, and only a few satisfy. Questions are necessary, valuable, unavoidable, a way to understand. Honesty is essential. (Turnage, 82)

Job's story is about loss of life, though not in the sense in which we typically use that phrase. The loss of life he knows and dreads is the loss of life as he has known it. He fears the loss of meaning and purpose to life, without which life is lost and becomes instead an uncertain number of empty days. "Why," he wonders, "is light given to one in misery, and life to the bitter in soul?" (v. 20). Job here seems for the first time to turn his attention to God. The passive voice of the question hides its subject, which it seems fair to assume is God. God is the creator of light and life. So why does the Creator create people for whom life is misery and bitterness, through no fault of their own? (Remember that we have the witness of God and ourselves that Job is blameless and upright.) If life is to be ultimately no more than suffering, why bother to give life in the first place?

Job searches for meaning in misery. His is a subtly but importantly different question than "Why do people suffer?" It asks, instead: Suppose life is no more than what Job knows now, suppose that its purpose were only suffering. Why would God create such a life? Why would God create life for misery and bitterness? The assumption of Job, in faith, has been that God creates life for good, that God has at heart the welfare of humankind and, for that matter, all creation. That assumption gives life meaning for Job and for us. But what if that's not true? What if God intends for us misery and suffering? What kind of meaning could there be in that? What if that's all there is to life?

Job's question is a profoundly disturbing one because it reaches to the core of his (and our) relationship to God. Job's faith and his experience contradict one another, maybe for the first time. His experience leads him to ask questions of his faith that he has never raised before. Indeed, while earlier he could accept both good and bad from the hand of God, Job has now changed; he is no longer compliant. The foundations of his trust in God have been shaken, forcing him to reconsider God's providence. He does not doubt, as we may, that God is responsible for the kind of life that now crushes him, but he wonders out loud what kind of steadfast loving God this is that creates life that is no more than suffering.

Job's question about meaning and purpose in life is continued in verse 23:

> [Why is light given] to one whose way is hidden,
>   whom God has hedged in?

> (my translation)

"Way" is a particularly important wisdom word, pointing to the path one should walk who would "fear God and turn from evil," as Job has done. It is a path, Proverbs especially affirms, that is well-known and requires only careful attention, observation, and the avoidance of evil to traverse. It is not an easy path, mind you. We might call it "the straight and narrow." But righteous persons, those who are God-fearing, are expected to stay its course. To do so is to live as God intends. Yet Job accuses God of blocking "the way," of intentionally hiding the path down which lies a full and happy life of peace and well-being. His faithful life should not have led to bitterness and misery, yet it has. The way ahead now is unclear; teaching has proved false to Job's experience. Now the righteous life lies hidden.

Moreover, Job is trapped, "hedged in" by God. The same image of hedging (or fencing) was used in chapter 1, you will recall, to describe God's protective surrounding of Job and his family. What was a surrounding fortress in the earlier passage has become a siege wall, imprisoning Job in his suffering. Wisdom taught that God intends humankind for a life of harmony with creation, one's neighbors, and one's self. Job can no longer see the way to life like that, and if living in such harmony provides life's meaning and purpose, then Job lives without either. Job holds God responsible for that and wonders if meaninglessness and purposelessness may be, in fact, the way God created life in the first place.

By the end of chapter 3, Job begins to perceive what he never could have imagined before: the enmity of God. Suffering has led him to this terrible possibility because there appears to him to be no other way of making sense of it. There is no place Job can see at the moment for undeserved suffering in his understanding of a loving and providential God.

The boldness of this image of enmity cannot be overstated. As the author sees it, the idea was new and traumatic for Job; it may be so for us as well. It would be easy to imagine Job abandoning God at this point in the story, even as God seems to have abandoned him. It would be easy to imagine people we know who suffer terribly abandoning God, and we would understand. Undeserved suffering stands as a sharp counterpoint to affirmations of God's love and care for us.

> Some people try to deal with the evil around them and in their own lives by pretending that it isn't there at all, or at least is not as bad as it seems. . . . Some of the worst injustice and suffering in the world is the result of "good" people simply refusing to acknowledge that evil exists and therefore doing nothing to challenge it. (Guthrie, 167)

Still, Job does not abandon God, nor does he cease trying to ground meaning and purpose in life in God's just ordering of creation. His integrity will not let him get to that end easily, though; his suffering requires him not to let go of God but to prepare to let go of his understanding of God, that is, his theology. Suffering leads Job to rethink what he has claimed to be true about God, human life, and himself. That may not be the test God and the Satan planned for Job, but it is the one he faces.

Ironically, then, accusing God is an act of faith. The hostility Job feels from God begins here softly, but it will build as the story does. Never, however, will Job "curse God and die." Never will he doubt that it is God with whom he must deal if he is to find the quiet and rest for which he so urgently longs. For the moment, however, Job's overwhelming feeling is one of bitter pain, divine betrayal, and a growing hostility between himself and God.

Theologian Dietrich Bonhoeffer once said, "I fear Christians rush too quickly to the New Testament. They need to read the Psalms first." Perhaps he had in mind particularly the lament psalms, the complaints of faithful people appealing for help to One who is often their oppressor, albeit also often for just cause. Striking for many of us is the bold, angry, and irreligious language and tone of the complaints. We are not accustomed to hearing voices raised in pain and protest against enemies and God. Our prayers seldom reflect the depths of anguish out of which the psalmist cries. Perhaps we think love will not bear such outrage or hostility. How strange it is when suffering speaks so softly in our presence, when it fairly shouts, cries out loud, and moans and groans in Israel's prayers and in Job's curses and complaint in chapter 3. I have known the crushing agony of which Job speaks, as many have, and I dare say we have shouted "God damn it!" to ourselves if no one else.

Some may admire the Job of chapters 1–2 more than the Job revealed in chapter 3, just as we may admire people we know who seem to accept their suffering quietly. We call them "amazing" and "an inspiration," "a steady rock." And well they may be, drawing their endurance from unfathomable resources. It could be that such remarkable people have made their peace with their suffering and found a place for understanding it in their lives.

As we now have Job's story, however, the person who once turned away suffering with wisdom sayings is the same one crying loudly and longing for death in chapter 3. These are not two images of response to undeserved suffering, as if we are asked to choose between them as a matter of faith. The message here is not that faithful people accept their suffering without question or are to be satisfied with the answer that "God gives and God takes away" (see Job 1:21). We see here, instead, the challenge that bone-deep suffering makes to faith for all of us, and we, like Job, may not respond consistently. Job found that his understanding of suffering, though sincerely held, would not bear the weight of his experience. Suffering is for Job and, I suspect for us, faith transforming. We let it be so by daring to admit the doubts and questions suffering forces on us.

For some, suffering leads to a reaffirmation of the faith they hold. For others, suffering forces a rethinking of faith. That is no less an act of faith and hope than the first scenario. God's love, we have learned, compels us to protest when life becomes unbearable. Moreover, God's love permits the full outrage of suffering seeking understanding, even if it means accusing God.

? Questions for Reflection

1. Have you ever said, "I wish I'd never been born"? Children sometimes say it out loud; adults may whisper it to themselves. What happened to you that brought you to that point?
2. Jesus, as well as Job, expressed feelings of abandonment by God (see Matt. 27:46). Have you ever had those feelings? What was that like? What did you do?
3. The author suggests that suffering can be a time for rethinking what one believes about God and meaning and purpose in life. How has suffering, yours or that of someone you love, challenged your faith?
4. Has there been a time when you have experienced deep suffering? Consider writing a poem or a prayer expressing what that is like. If you are comfortable doing so, share it with others.

3 Job 6:1–7:21

In the Image of God

After chapter 3, soliloquy turns to dialogue as Job's friends respond to his outcries and arguments. Chapters 3–27 build the dialogue in three cycles of verbal exchange between Job and each of the friends in turn. For example, Eliphaz speaks first (chaps. 4–5) in response to Job's curse against the day of his birth (chap. 3). Job, in turn, responds to Eliphaz (chaps. 6–7) before Bildad adds his perspective to the discussion (chap. 8). Job then responds to Bildad (chaps. 9–10). Then Zophar takes his turn at arguing with Job's claims (chap. 11), and so on until three rounds of alternating speeches are completed. The reader should be aware that there are irregularities in the third cycle, where Bildad's speech seems remarkably brief as it stands, and Zophar's expected speech is not clearly present at all. The three cycles that constitute the whole dialogue are structured as follows:

Cycle 1: chapters 4–14
Cycle 2: chapters 15–21
Cycle 3: chapters 22–27

A fourth friend, Elihu, appears suddenly near the end of the book to address both Job and the other three friends in a very long speech (chaps. 32–37). Job, however, never responds to him, nor do any of the three friends. Nevertheless, Elihu's arguments are clearly related to those of the dialogue cycles though not a part of them.

I recently watched a debate between two candidates for political office, and it occurred to me that what I was witnessing was not unlike the character of the dialogues between Job and the friends— not in content, of course, but in form. The structure of the debate called for each candidate to respond to questions posed by a moderator, with each then having an opportunity for rebuttal of the opponent's argument. A technique that struck me was the ability of each candidate to use the opponent's words as a means of getting to the case the speaker wanted to make in the first place. Picking up on one or two words or even a single concept offered by the first speaker, the second speaker would glance off the other's words, responding indirectly to the argument, in order to get to her point.

The dialogue in Job is a bit like that. Speeches often do not directly address perspectives raised by a previous speaker. More often, catchwords and images from one speaker may be taken up by another and sometimes turned on their head in a new argument. Job often begins speaking to the one who has addressed him, then, as in a soliloquy, he suddenly speaks directly to God or to himself. Also, like a political candidate, the same themes appear in multiple speeches. Particularly that is true for the friends, who argue with maddening consistency the traditional views of God's justice and the consequent reasons for Job's suffering, without granting the possibility of an

> The problem is precisely that Job is a "good" man whose lot is *not* prosperity, but suffering. The "friends" can solve the problem only by denying that it exists. Since badness = suffering, Job must be bad. Period. Case dismissed. But the book presents Job as an upright, righteous man. The formula, in other words, doesn't always work. (Brown 1955, 146)

alternative view to Job at all. The result for the listener (or reader) is the sense that the friends and Job are speaking *past* one another rather than *to* one another, making it difficult to see their speeches as a genuine dialogue.

On the other hand, this pattern of speaking that I have sketched is appropriate for the struggle that is going on within Job. The author has crafted a dialogue that is shaped by the emotional level of the story. The friends' perspective represents the orthodox point of view of Job's day—one which, as chapters 1–2 indicate, Job shared until his experience of overwhelming suffering shook the foundations of his traditional faith. Each of Job's speeches struggles toward making sense of a personal crisis that seems senseless and destructive of Job's very relationship with God. But always he must argue, so to speak, against himself, against the way he has always understood God's ordering of the world, the nature of God's justice, and the relationship of human behavior to a good and well-blessed life. His experience challenges what he has believed to be true, and the traditional view in which he once took solace now goads him toward some new way of seeing how things truly are. Job cannot accept the old way anymore, but an alternative still lies beyond his grasp, so the dialogue carries the old perspective along in the hands of his friends even as a new way of seeing is being forged.

Is that not the way it is for us too? When experience calls to question what we have long held to be true, we find ourselves trapped for a while between what we know we don't believe any longer and what we may come to believe. These are threshold moments, and we let go of past views only with reluctance and a sense of disequilibrium as we stretch toward a new perspective that can take our experience into account. "I don't know what I believe any longer," confessed a friend of mine whose wife had recently died of brain cancer after seven long years of agony. "I believe in God," he went on, "but after that, I don't know. Nothing makes any sense any longer." Job stands at a threshold like this, and so, perhaps, may we.

The chapters we are studying in this session, chapters 6–7, represent Job's retort to Eliphaz (chaps. 4–5). The dramatic and outrageous language of Job in chapter 3 leaves the reader unprepared for Eliphaz's rather restrained and polite opening to his response.

> If one ventures a word with you, will you be offended?
> But who can keep from speaking?
>
> (4:2)

In the face of Job's damning outcry against the day of his birth and, finally, against God, Eliphaz is constrained to speak. He and his friends have come to "condole and comfort" Job, and Eliphaz in this speech will offer comfort by reminding Job of what he has always taken to be true. As one who knows the wisdom tradition well, he appeals to community experience as well as doctrine. He offers Job similar advice to that which Job himself has given to those in need of support and encouragement to keep them on the straight and narrow path to the good life (4:3–4). He argues:

> Is not your fear of God your confidence,
> and the integrity of your ways your hope?
> Think now, who that was innocent ever perished?
> Or where were the upright cut off?
> As I have seen, those who plow iniquity
> and sow trouble reap the same.
>
> (4:6–8)

Job should be able to take refuge in his beliefs and place his hope in the upright life he has lived. His behavior has a promised outcome that is inscribed in God's moral ordering of life. If he holds fast to his integrity (with which God, the Satan, and his wife credit him in chaps. 1–2), then his future is assured. Eliphaz warns him against impatience and angry speech, however, like that of his outburst that sought to upend creation.

As for Job's suffering, Eliphaz raises two possibilities for understanding it that do not undermine the traditional affirmation that the righteous are blessed and the wicked punished. First, he reports to Job a message received as revelation that suggests that no created being can stand before God in total innocence (4:12–21). Human beings are like clay houses, with their foundations in dust (4:19), which are easily destroyed. Suffering, then, may come as a result of being a human creature. The creature is not the Creator, after all, and cannot stand on the same moral plane with the Almighty. Implicitly, then, Job's innocence must be relative in relationship to God's righteousness. What mortal can question God's righteousness or the purity of God's intentions? Job is a creature of earth and subject to all human frailties. As the Protestant Reformers insisted, by his nature, Job cannot be totally free of sin, nor can any of us be. Job and we must live always within the bounds of our creatureliness and thus within the generosity of God's forgiving grace. Eliphaz's argument is an invitation to humility for Job and for us.

Eliphaz's second argument that would explain Job's suffering posits a purpose to suffering. In this case, it is not simply accidental to being human but an intentional effort at instruction initiated by God. Drawing on wisdom tradition, Eliphaz reminds Job:

> How happy is the one whom God reproves;
>> therefore do not despise the discipline of the Almighty.
> For he wounds, but he binds up;
>> he strikes, but his hands heal.

> (5:17–18)

Job, then, should not condemn either his suffering or God. His suffering is intended to "discipline" him. *How* pain instructs Eliphaz does not say. He seeks less to explain Job's condition than to affirm God's ultimate good intention. Job should accept his suffering as a student accepts discipline from a wise teacher or a child from a parent, with trust that the teacher has the best interest of the learner at heart. A long life lived in conformity with God's way, the way of wisdom, is the purpose of such discipline and, indeed, its promised outcome—a fact Eliphaz offers Job as a comforting reminder.

Eliphaz's speech is punctuated with praise for God, who "does great things" and "marvelous things without number" (5:9; see also vv. 10–16). Job's time of discipline will not last forever. God, Eliphaz assures Job, will deliver him and restore him to a life of peace and security, for that is the nature of God's relationship to humankind. Eliphaz's praise celebrates a faithful, steadfast, caring, and nurturing God. Implicit in his praise is a call for Job to seek God and trust God in spite of Job's suffering and to refrain from such foolish talk as he has already exhibited. He has already come close to cursing God. He must, instead, "commit [his] cause to God" (5:8).

> Job's physical suffering pales in comparison with his mental agony over this unfathomable face of God, which no longer smiles on him but now contorts itself angrily before him. It seems to Job that this God actively destroys all hope, wearing it away like the slow erosion of rocks brought about by flowing water. (Crenshaw, 97–98)

Job responds with anger and sarcasm, aimed first at Eliphaz and his companions and then at God (chaps. 6–7). If Eliphaz's psalms are those of praise and thanksgiving, Job's response mirrors psalms of unrelenting lament and accusation. These two chapters represent what Carol Newsom wryly calls "Job's anti-psalms" (Newsom 1996, 398). They seem carefully drawn to mock the hymnic character of Eliphaz's speech and to counter his advice to Job to "seek God" and be restored.

Job has spoken "rashly" (6:3) because the weight of his disaster demands no less. More controlled speech, advocated by the wise, does not fit his situation, the critical character of which Eliphaz does not seem to grasp. Far from the image of a caring teacher wanting the best for her students and disciplining them for the sake of a better, richer life, Job's image of God is that of an enemy warrior, attacking him with poisoned arrows designed not to teach but to kill body and soul (6:4).

Far from seeking God for comfort, Job finds only pain and estrangement in his relationship with God. His hope lies not in God's care and promise of restoration but in being "cut off" and "crushed" by God so that he is no longer the victim of his hostility (6:8–9). Job has no more strength for waiting. Eliphaz's words bring no consolation, with their appeal to traditional values, unfounded optimism, and hint that Job's suffering is the result of sin. Job finds his consolation not in the friends, though that was their purpose for coming to him, but in the honesty with which he has spoken of God's "decrees" against him (6:10). Verse 10 is notoriously difficult to translate. Here I read with Habel's translation:

> This would be my comfort;
> I would revel amid relentless pain,
> Because I will not have concealed the decrees of the Holy One.
>
> (Habel 1985, 138)

The very language for which Eliphaz chides Job is what keeps him going in the midst of his suffering. Implicit in the play on words that is visible in the phrase "decrees of God" is a countercharge against Eliphaz that his way of describing God's words is dishonest in Job's particular case. Job cannot tone it down; the pain is too immense and the injustice too plain. Urgent speech is often reckless. And Job's life hangs in the balance.

> Therefore I will not restrain my mouth;
> I will speak in the anguish of my spirit;
> I will complain in the bitterness of my soul.
>
> (7:11)

From defending himself, Job switches to accusing Eliphaz and his friends. Indeed, argues Job, they are not friends worthy of the name (6:14–30). True friends would remain loyal even if Job seems no longer able to embrace the traditional beliefs that they do. Yet in the wake of his protests against life and against God, these "friends" are ready to abandon him, eager to separate themselves from him and his reckless outbursts. In a telling and devastating metaphor, Job accuses them of being like a desert wadi that runs fresh with water in the rainy season only to dry up just when parched travelers seek its comfort and sustenance. When he needs their nourishment most, the friends give Job nothing but empty dust and failed promises.

> Such you have now become to me;
> you see my calamity, and are afraid.
>
> (6:21)

Yet Job has not asked that they risk anything for him. They came to him proclaiming their friendship, but now they attack him and accuse him of foolish and unfaithful behavior. They are, Job suggests, nothing but fair-weather friends, which means not true friends at all.

33

Eliphaz has spoken in platitudes and warned Job to temper his speech, but no one has revealed to Job what terrible thing he has done wrong that could possibly justify the extent of his suffering. Eliphaz's words, instead, prove nothing and simply "blow off" Job's distress call (6:26). Far from being friends, Eliphaz and the others act without human compassion, as if casting lots over an orphan or haggling over a friend's life (6:27). What Job needs right now are friends who can show compassionate love, not critics—friends who can be counted on to join him in his anguish and protest his suffering, who can encourage his grief and stand open to his struggle for language that can comprehend his condition. Instead, he gets from Eliphaz (and the author suggests the rest as well) reproof: How can you talk this way? What's happened to you? Where's your faith? These are words of chastisement, not comfort, not acceptance, and not compassion. With friends like these, Job might say now, who needs enemies?

Ignoring the "friends," Job now turns to face God. While his words are biting and sarcastic—a radically different tone than even in the lament psalms—that he addresses God at all places his bitter speech in the context of faith. Job does not abandon God, here or elsewhere in the book, despite his feeling that God has abandoned their relationship and become the enemy. Eliphaz had ventured a description of the human condition, arguing that we are creatures of dust and subject to all the uncertainties that finite existence entails. In chapter 7, Job offers his own take on the human condition. Human life, he declares, is short, no more than a breath. It passes quickly, "swifter than a weaver's shuttle," and comes to an end without hope (7:6). The thread simply runs out. And there is no more. These are days of "hard service," the Hebrew suggesting here "military service" and constant embattlement. They are days of little reward, like those of a day laborer awaiting his daily pay. Job's life is the worse yet because his few days are full of pain, so that even the promise of a night's rest has become a bitter joke. This picture of God's "gift" of life could not be further from Eliphaz's vision of God's generosity. This is not just crea-

Want to Know More?

About Job's debate with his friends? See Robert McAfee Brown, *The Bible Speaks to You* (Philadelphia: Westminster Press, 1955), 144–49; and Carol A. Newsom, "Job," in *The Women's Bible Commentary*, ed. Carol A. Newsom and Sharon H. Ringe (Louisville, Ky.: Westminster/John Knox Press, 1992), 132–133.

About depression as a spiritual crisis? See Thomas Lewis, *Finding God: Praying the Psalms in Times of Depression* (Louisville, Ky.: Westminster John Knox Press, 2002), chap. 3.

turely accident but planned oppression, and God is the creator of it and responsible for it.

Job is not the victim of a terrible mistake; he is God's victim, the target of God's cruelty. God is hounding Job to death. Job upends the image of traditional faith that perceives God as a constant and loving protector, whose presence is blessing and peace. Job's image of God is that of a constant watcher, one who constantly scrutinizes human life, looking for the slightest weakness, in whose presence life becomes bearable only if God looks away.

Job 7:17–18 offers a condemning parody on Psalm 8, that high-minded and celebratory song about God's "mindfulness" of human beings. Expressing his amazement that God could make so much of human beings within the grandeur of all creation, the psalmist sings:

> Yet you have made them a little lower than God,
>   and crowned them with glory and honor.
> You have given them dominion over the works of your hands;
>   you have put all things under their feet.
> . . . .
> O LORD, our Sovereign,
>   how majestic is your name in all the earth!
>
> (Ps. 8:5–6, 9)

Job too is amazed that God "makes so much" of human beings. Gone, however, is the celebration of God's generosity toward human beings, who are painted in royal colors and given dominion over all creation. Job's picture is not that of royalty but of human beings constantly visited, not for care but for affliction and testing (7:18). So intense is God's harassment of humankind that Job begs:

> Will you not look away from me for a while,
>   let me alone until I swallow my spittle?
>
> (7:19)

Why, Job questions, if human beings are creatures who sin and who stand far from the righteousness of God, does God care so much about human error? Why not simply forgive it? What harm could it possibly do to one as majestic and pure as God, whose righteousness is always beyond human reach? Instead, God seems ready to pursue Job to his death; then, ironically, when God wants him, Job will no longer exist (7:20–21). Job's God is not majestic but mean-spirited, like a cosmic bully constantly picking on weaker kids, heckling, hitting, and making someone else's life miserable, until, in the end, the victim finally disappears. Then the game is no fun any longer, since watching the victim suffer was part of its attraction.

Job's response to Eliphaz in these two chapters asks at least two profound questions of us. First, it asks about the character of true friendship. What does it mean to be a friend, and what do we rightly expect of our friends? More particularly, Job asks us to think about how we befriend someone who is suffering and what the things we say and do may feel like to one whose ordinary way of seeing has been blurred by being blindsided by tragedy.

Stories from congregational life and from personal life abound of people being good friends and neighbors in times of crisis. Food appears for nourishment as well as comfort; someone offers to keep up the necessary routines no longer on the horizon of a suffering friend. In the face of tragedy, even good friends may find it hard to know just what to say or do to help beyond "I'm sorry. Is there anything I (we) can do?" The core complaint Job had with his "friends" is that they expected certain standard behavior from him, and when

The deepest friendship involves compassion, loyalty, and love.

he failed to conform to their expectations, their "comforting" became finding ways to "correct" Job and thereby make themselves more comfortable. What he expected from them, if we may read between the lines—and, I dare say, what our suffering friends expect of us— is room in the relationship to express one's deepest feelings, particularly those of anger and frustration and injustice, or to remain silent, if one so chooses. Job expects them to respect his perspective, radically changed though it may be, and not let their own fear try to silence his outrage.

Suffering compels us to rethink even our deepest held convictions, and we need friends who can allow that to happen and be loyal companions along the way to a new point of view, no matter how rugged the going gets or how much it conflicts with their own perspective.

Suffering friends are not comforted by correction but by compassion, which joins, as much as possible, in the suffering, to provide a source of strength and resistance so that life becomes bearable and, eventually perhaps, even hopeful. Befriending another is a holy calling, because such loyalty and love becomes the way by which the compassion of God may be experienced by all of us and especially by those whose need for it is urgent. Job, sadly, found neither in his exchange with Eliphaz and the other friends.

The other important question these chapters ask us concerns our view of what it means to be human. Who are we and, most especially, who are we in relationship to God? Are we the blessed and privileged creatures the author of Psalm 8 imagines, "made in the image of God," given dominion over all God has made? Or are we nearer to the portrait Job paints of our relationship to God, pursued by God persistently, not for good but to test the strength of our character and our ability to withstand the scrutiny of God? Which image does your experience uphold? Job poses the question in the starkest way possible, and perhaps it is too stark for us.

Perhaps we would want to protest that neither image suits us well. We are creatures with whom God has graciously covenanted in Christ; we are redeemed sinners, fearfully and wonderfully made in the image of God. And the image of God we know is Jesus Christ, an image of love overcoming hate and life overcoming death. Created by God, we are valued by God, forgiven by God, and loved by God eternally. It is not an easy declaration, mind you. Inhumanity must still be accounted for, and tragedy still begs for faithful understanding. The truth of our confession is not always easy to see, measured on the plane of human experience. The very magnanimity of faith's vision provides room to doubt its truth in the face of tragedy and acute suffering. Faith sets high standards not just for human beings to live up to but also for God to meet. And we are not wrong, in the midst of suffering, to hold both God and ourselves accountable.

? Questions for Reflection

1. Eliphaz offers two explanations for human suffering: the inherently sinful nature of being human and God's discipline of us. How satisfying to you are these two ways of accounting for suffering? Why does Job reject them?

2. Think of someone who was a good friend to you or to someone whom you loved in a time of great suffering. How was friendship shown? How was the nonsufferer able to create space for the suffering one's anger and doubts and tears?

3. Read Psalm 8, then reread Job 7:17–18. Which of these portraits of the human condition resonates most with you? Why?

4. Have there been times in your life when God has seemed more an enemy than a caring friend? What were those times like and how did you deal with your feelings?

Holding God Accountable

In these two chapters, Job begins to develop an image that will become increasingly important through the rest of the book. It is triggered by a rhetorical question posed by Bildad, the second friend, whose response to Job's argument with Eliphaz appears in chapter 8. For the most part, Bildad has little new to say, and what he does add seems callous and cold. Like Eliphaz, he does not accuse Job directly of being guilty of anything that would justify his suffering. Instead, Bildad proclaims that if Job's children sinned, then they got what they deserved. As for Job, Bildad repeats Eliphaz's advice to seek God and "make supplication" to him, in the confidence that if he is blameless and upright, "[God] will rouse himself for you" and Job will be restored to his "rightful place" (8:4–7). Appealing to the wisdom of those who have gone before them, he repeats the orthodoxy regarding the disastrous fate of the wicked and the corresponding happy condition of the righteous.

Early in his speech, however, as he rebukes Job for "blowing off" like a great wind, he poses this question:

> Does God pervert justice?
> Or does the Almighty pervert the right?
>
> (8:3)

The question is rhetorical, and Bildad expects to find common ground with Job in a negative response—"Of course God does not pervert justice"—but Job is not buying the easy answer. In chapters 9–10, Job takes Bildad's query as an open question. Job's suffering seems to be an instance of God perverting justice, since Job, God, and the reader know that Job is blameless and upright. Eliphaz, also in a rhetorical question, had asked Job,

> Can mortals be righteous before God?
> Can human beings be pure before their Maker?
>
> (4:17)

Job begins his speech in chapter 9 with words almost identical: "How can a mortal be just before God?" Or, as a rhetorical question expecting a negative reply, we could translate, "A human being cannot be in the right before God." Job's concern, unlike Eliphaz, is not with morality. Sparked by Bildad's introduction of the issue of divine justice, Job turns Eliphaz's question about morality into a legal issue. No one, Job suggests, could get a fair trial with God. More radically still, he contends, no one can successfully bring charges against God or expect due process in a court where God stands as accuser and accused. Job's answer to Bildad's question, in a word, is "Yes, God *does* pervert justice, and I am a case in point."

In these chapters, the author of Job, through what Gerald Janzen calls "imaginative outreach" (Janzen, 70), begins to consider what would happen if someone as violated as Job sought justice by bringing charges against the one responsible for doing justice in heaven and on earth. Job begins to imagine a scene in a court where a trial against God is being held, where he could present his case against his tormentor and hear, for the first time, God's complaint against him. The chapters are full of juridical references, harder to see in English than in Hebrew. For example, the word for "righteous" (9:2) in its forensic sense means "be in the right," and the word translated "contend" suggests "going to trial" (9:3). On the surface, the idea is ludicrous, as Job himself admits:

> For he is not a mortal, as I am, that I might answer him,
> that we should come to trial together.
>
> (9:32)

God's servant Job would become a litigant in a case to hold God accountable for Job's destruction "without reason" (2:3). Who could find God "guilty," though? It bends the mind.

Yet it is human experience. In his preface to Holocaust survivor Elie Wiesel's play *The Trial of God*, Robert McAfee Brown recounts the incident in Wiesel's tortured experience as a twelve-year-old in the

Nazi death camp of Auschwitz that gave rise to the play. Wiesel became the only witness one night to a remarkable event. Three great Jewish scholars put God on trial, "creating in that eerie place a rabbinic court of law to indict the Almighty." The trial lasted several nights, during which evidence was presented and witnesses testified until finally there was a unanimous verdict: "[T]he Lord God Almighty, Creator of Heaven and Earth, was found guilty of crimes against creation and humankind" (Brown 1995, vii)—a desperate act for desperate times when suffering reached immeasurable proportions for six million Jews and countless other victims of Nazi cruelty and dehumanization. The trial that night was an act of faith and an act of protest against a just and loving God who could, nonetheless, allow people whom God loved to be torn from their homes, tortured and violated, and finally destroyed. Our question "Why?" begs God to justify our senseless suffering and the betrayal of a promise to be with us and care for us.

> There are those who claim that all suffering comes from God. This is simply a crueler version of the notion that all suffering is punishment for sin. (Brown 1955, 148)

With our painful plea for a response from God, we come close to bringing charges against God ourselves. To find God guilty, however, requires a huge measure of faith, for it disallows any escape to mysterious purposes and reasons.

Keep in mind that Job's worldview reflects that of his society, as mentioned earlier. That means that he shares in the wisdom of his day, affirming that right and wrong and their consequences constitute an order of justice that is laced through God's creation. God has granted human beings a measure of wisdom that allows us to discern this pattern and to shape our lives in accordance with it. Therefore, men and women are accountable to it. Job's friends have taken a step beyond this perspective and treat the condition of one's life as evidence of guilt or innocence, wickedness or righteousness. They would make the pattern of justice reversible, which ignores the multiple reasons why a person may be poor or rich, happy or despairing. Their bad logic leads them to insist that Job's condition is justified by something Job has done to deserve it. They grant that Job may not know what it is that he has done, but they have no doubt something in his behavior has brought his present desperate condition about.

Job, however, takes a different turn, though assuming the same pattern of justice in creation as do the friends. With the introduction of the trial metaphor, he introduces the contention that God must be accountable to God's own order of justice. Job, in his integrity, insists

41

that he is innocent and poses the possibility that, since he is innocent, God is guilty of violating his own justice. He concludes, therefore, that there is no justice at all, if not even God acts justly. Job does not assume that all suffering is unjust. He knows, as we do, that some suffering we bring on ourselves, through poor decisions, the violence we perpetrate against others and ourselves, and poor self-care. On the other hand, we may also be victims of violence, of poverty and poor living conditions, or of hazardous or toxic materials in our environment. Human beings are behind these actions as well.

Yet in Job's worldview, these are all secondary causes. At the very least, God allows them to happen; at the very worst, God is the perpetrator of violence. In either case, from Job's point of view, God stands indictable. Since God is ultimately responsible for human suffering, God bears the burden of showing how suffering is justified. The trial metaphor points to Job's deep desire to know how God could justify the destruction of his family and his way of life, subject him to painful sores that will not let him find a moment's peace, and stand by watching him waste away. A trial could force an answer: a charge against Job that would justify his enormous suffering or an admission on God's part that there is nothing to justify it. God only knows.

How does a human being carry on a lawsuit (9:3; NRSV, "contend") against God? We know relatively little about the judicial process in ancient Israel. Apparently no distinction was made between civil and criminal trials, which took place ordinarily "in the gate" of the city. Complaints were brought to the elders sitting in the gate, before whom the aggrieved party made his case. The respondent also had an opportunity to speak, and witnesses were called. The elder(s) rendered a decision subsequently. Ruth 4:1–12 provides a glimpse into this legal process, in a case that is less a dispute than the settlement of a legal agreement. The legal process assumed equality between parties involved, a mutual standard of justice, and the impartiality and wisdom of the elders hearing the case.

Job imagines facing God in court, trying to make a case against God for a violation of justice, and having to respond to God's counterclaims. The overwhelming power of God makes the process seem futile to Job at first. In an ironic twist, he offers a psalm praising God's creative power that mirrors Eliphaz's hymn in 5:8–16. Job's psalm, however, takes note of the destructive and disruptive power of the Creator (9:4–13). Ordinarily, the "shaking of the foundations" pictured here is in behalf of God's people against an enemy, but for Job the image characterizes a battle fought against him. He has become God's enemy. Unlike Eliphaz's experience of a passing spirit and a divine revelation (4:12–21), Job experiences God as distant and mute:

> Look, he passes by me, and I do not see him;
>   he moves on, but I do not perceive him.
> He snatches away; who can stop him?
>   Who will say to him, "What are you doing?"
>
>   (9:11–12)

God, in Job's view, holds all the cards. And Job seems to have little choice than to beg for mercy from his apparent accuser, even though he is innocent.

> If I summoned him and he answered me,
>   I do not believe that he would listen to my voice.
> For he crushes me with a tempest,
>   and multiplies my wounds without cause;
> he will not let me get my breath,
>   but fills me with bitterness.
>
>   (9:16–18)

He concludes:

> If it is a contest of strength, he is the strong one!
>   If it is a matter of justice, who can summon him?
>
>   (9:19)

Justice, Job argues, is nonexistent. The behavior of God compels this conclusion:

> It is all one; therefore I say,
>   he destroys both the blameless and the wicked.
> . . . .
> The earth is given into the hand of the wicked;
>   he covers the eyes of its judges—
>   if it is not he, who then is it?
>
>   (9:22, 24)

There is no hope for a fair hearing when God is not accountable to God's own code of justice.

What alternatives are there if Job is to have some explanation for the injustice he has suffered at the hands of God, for God's continued torment, and apparent mockery of innocent suffering? He considers as one option simply forgetting his case against God, repressing his despair, washing his face, and getting on with his life (9:27–29). Ignoring his suffering is not a real option, however; it is too dreadful to allow living normally. Moreover, a change in his behavior would make no difference, since God seems to have found him guilty already, despite his innocence. Ignoring his protest of innocence before God is futile; it would accomplish nothing. He is like a prisoner before a judge who has already made up his mind to find the defendant guilty, regardless of evidence to the contrary. So what's the use?

> Could it be that sometimes God seems so far away because we look for God's presence only when things go well, when problems are solved and questions answered; and do not look for it where God also promises to be present with us—where everything falls apart in our own lives and in the world around us? (Guthrie, 187)

Perhaps, Job thinks, though innocent, a rite of purification would satisfy his accuser (9:30–31), but that is not likely, either. God would simply plunge him deeper into filth, transforming his inner cleansing into an outward, putrid smell of death, making him appear all the more guilty. Rather than the clean garments of innocence, his filthy rags would condemn him (see Habel 1985, 196). Job has lost any sense of a compassionate and caring God. God seems to Job only bent on making things worse for him. His desperation leads him to one final hope. If only someone could be found to mediate a hearing between God and Job, someone who could stand between a mortal and the Almighty and see to a fair trial, then Job could speak without fear and argue his innocence. There is no one like that, though. It is an empty hope.

So Job returns to consider bringing God to justice through a lawsuit that names God as the defendant. He imagines what he would say to God if such a hearing were possible (10:1–17). His scathing indictment accuses God of oppression, of incessant pursuit and surveillance in an effort to catch Job in some wrongdoing, and of taking advantage of Job, knowing that there is no one to deliver him from God's crushing action against him. Finally, Job accuses God of intentionally destroying the very work of his creation that Job is, and of intending his degradation all along, as if he were made for it by a perverse Creator who takes pleasure in the suffering of what he makes. The image of God that comes to mind for me with Job's indictment is that of young children painstakingly building a city of blocks or Tinkertoys, only to smash their creation in the end, with squeals of delight. It is a shocking contrast to the image of a just God, who saves the oppressed, stands at the side of those who are vulnerable, who sees to the basic needs of the whole created order, and who delights, as the prophet Amos declared, when "justice roll[s] down like waters, and righteousness like an everflowing stream" (Amos 5:24).

His practiced trial speech completed, Job is once more struck by the futility of the creature demanding justice from his creator. God seems free of God's own justice. So Job returns at the close of chapter 10 to themes familiar from his anguished lament of chapter 3. Unlike the lament of that chapter, however, this one addresses God directly. Nor does a longing for death absorb the lament, as it did previously. Rather, Job seeks relief from the day-to-day agony of soul and body he suffers:

> Are not the days of my life few?
>> Let me alone that I may find a little comfort
> before I go, never to return,
>> to the land of gloom and deep darkness,
> the land of gloom and chaos,
>> where light is like darkness.

> (10:20–22)

It is a sad prayer. Job does not ask for the saving or comforting presence of God. He asks instead for God to look away and leave him alone. Comfort comes, Job believes, in the absence of God rather than the presence of God. Still, the prayer is offered *to* God, and any hope Job has remains with God. He cannot hope for forgiveness, because there is no failure to be forgiven. He cannot hope for vindication, because the keeper of justice is not bound by it. He can only hope for a truce of sorts that allows for a respite of his suffering— small comfort, slim hope, but hope nonetheless.

Job's cry for a lawsuit that would bring God into court with him is, at heart, a plea for reconciliation with God. That is why the image of God as the destroying Creator is so painful to Job. As it is, Job's relationship with God seems irreparably broken. He cannot imagine what he could possibly have done to set God against him. The lawsuit is a hope to set things right, to plead his case with God, arguing his innocence, in order to persuade God to reestablish their relationship. It is important to Job—and one would think to God—that it be a relationship of integrity. For that reason, Job continues to insist on his innocence, and he expects God to be accountable to God's commitments to justice and the well-being of those whom he has created. God is our protector from chaos, from the overflow of destructive forces in our lives. Job images such chaos in his charge against God: "He destroys both the blameless and the wicked" (9:22). If there is to be a new relationship, from Job's point of view, either God must show him what he has done that justifies God becoming an adversary, or God must make a case that somehow justifies innocent suffering. Whichever the case, it is essential to be made, in Job's view, if a trusting relationship is to be forged again.

Job's hope for a confrontation with God before an impartial judge participates in an experience that many sufferers know. Inside suffering there is a kind of emotive thinking that can imagine dialogues with the self or with others or with suffering personified that would make little sense to those on the outside of the experience. From the inside, however, they make perfectly good sense, because suffering has a logic of its own. In the midst of many "dark nights of the soul," I recall vividly one-sided conversations I had with God, who somehow—I knew not how—held the keys to understanding and escaping my torment. I pleaded with God to tell me what I had done to deserve the darkness all around me and, simultaneously, to take it away. "Where is the justice in my suffering?" I asked God. I felt betrayed and said so, implicitly asking God to defend God's self. Always there was silence. In my right mind, I would not have talked like that, even to myself. The questions were not abstract to me. In my turbulent mind, these diatribes were ways of fighting back, of doing something to keep from falling further and further into the pit. They were grabbing, clutching fingers at the edge of an abyss, trying to pull free.

Suffering makes us strangers to ourselves and often to others. And we, like Job, may feel estranged from God as well. In the context of suffering, calling God to account is far from blasphemy. It is an act of faith in search of God's steadfast love.

? Questions for Reflection

1. What does it mean to you to say that God is just? How is God's justice experienced in life?
2. Job's friends believed that those who suffer must have done something to deserve it. In our own pain, we too may ask, "What did I

do to deserve this?" What would you say to someone who asked you that question?

3. Try to imagine that you were to take God to court. What charges would you bring against God? How would the indictment read?

4. Is Job justified in holding God accountable for innocent suffering? Why or why not?

5 Job 12:1-14:22

Job's Impossible Dream

This is Job's fourth speech, and the longest of them all. Most immediately, it is Job's response to Zophar, the third friend to engage Job in loud and impassioned argument.

It comes at a pivotal place in Job's story, marking the end of the first cycle of speeches. So it is not surprising that Job's response to Zophar is, in fact, addressed to all three of his so-called friends. In this speech, they are the focus of 12:1–13:19, at which point Job turns his back on them to address God (13:20–14:22). Job's emotions run the gamut here. He is angry, caustic, determined, plaintive, aggressive, and tender, a man on an emotional roller coaster from start to finish.

The friends have come to Job to console him, to offer their sympathy and understanding, and to share, insofar as they may, in his disfiguring suffering. Yet Eliphaz, Bildad, and now Zophar have each been drawn into rancorous dispute with the one whom they have come to comfort. What has "hooked" each one of them has been Job's near blasphemous accusations against God and insistent protest that he is innocent of any wrongdoing that could possibly justify God's imposition of such unimaginable grief and pain as Job suffers. They are each determined to convince him of his wrongheaded claims and to demonstrate to him how he can make sense of his plight and recover from it.

The pressing tone of their arguments, we may imagine, arises from two critical concerns. First—and we must take their efforts here as genuine care—they fear that Job is denying himself God-given resources for his healing and restoration which his faith tradition puts squarely before him, namely, the promise of God's mercy and forgiveness in response to an admission of wrongdoing. "There is," they plead, "a way out of your suffering, Job. Admit the error of your ways

48

and trust God to restore you." Job steadfastly denies these theological physicians' diagnosis and prescription. Indeed, he calls them here "worthless physicians" (13:4). There is nothing to confess, Job contends; moreover, God is not to be trusted. Far from being bent on Job's healing, God is, from Job's point of view, committed to his destruction. That suggests the friends' second cause for their urgent attack on Job's "ravings." Job's conclusions about God's enmity and injustice toward human beings in general and himself in particular threaten the friends' traditional beliefs, Job's denial of which they take very personally. Job's arguments challenge what they believe, indeed, what they hold to be unassailably true about God, what is right and wrong, and how God has ordered life.

To get close to the friends' feelings we need only remember the impassioned and often uncivil fights that take place in the church over beliefs we take to be central and nonnegotiable to a "right understanding of faith." Matters of faith and the ways we express what we believe are of ultimate importance to us. No wonder our rhetoric gets passionate and we sometimes feel attacked—theology matters! And it matters to each of us deeply. No less is the case for Job and the friends. The friends' words are biting, but no less than Job's own. Their intention to comfort seems a long way off in their angry and cutting remarks to Job. There is more than Job's suffering at stake from the friends' point of view; there is the honor of God and right and wrong belief in the balance.

Detail from the lower panel of the sarcophagus of Junius Bassus, a Roman prefect who died in 359 CE, showing Job and his three friends— Grotte Vaticane, Vatican City, and Vatican.

Zophar mocks the supposed wisdom of Job, chiding him for claiming to know better than God. He appeals to the mystery of God's wisdom, which he describes as "many-sided" and beyond Job's comprehension. He presses Job to abandon his arrogance: "Can you find out the deep things of God? Can you find out the limit of the Almighty?" (11:7), he asks rhetorically. If you knew as much as you *think* you know, you would know that "God exacts of you less than your guilt deserves" (11:6), Zophar argues. Zophar remains locked in his traditional theological formula: Job's suffering must have

a cause grounded in his wrongdoing. Far from passing Job by without seeing him (see 9:11–12), God's limitless wisdom penetrates the
deepest recesses of Job's being:

> If [God] passes through, and imprisons,
>   and assembles for judgment, who can hinder him?
> For he knows those who are worthless;
>   when he sees iniquity, will he not consider it?

>   (11:10–11)

Zophar's implication is clear enough: Job is a fool (the meaning of
"worthless") claiming wisdom on a par with God. Job's hope lies not
in his claim to innocence, as he insists, but in humility before God,
in "getting right" with God (11:13). Then God will grant him the
relief and rest he so desperately seeks. That too is part of the mystery
of God's wisdom.

   In the abstract, Zophar's argument is not unattractive, setting aside
for the moment his biting personal attack on Job. After all, Zophar
and his two companions represent a perspective that, until very
recently, had been Job's as well. They are, as it were, Job's alter ego.
God's wisdom *is* mysterious and beyond human comprehension,
even if we may know something of what God knows. And Job's
protest of his innocence *does* strike us as at least bordering on arrogance; no one, we think, is that good. In fact, if nothing more, perhaps it is Job's stubborn protest against God that constitutes his
wrongdoing. Finally, we *do* want to affirm that God, no matter how
just the judgment, is eager to forgive and restore any who reach out
for forgiveness. The wisdom of God, while finally unknowable, is
totally reliable—we want to believe that. That is where our hope, our
confidence rests—in the gracious character of an infinitely wise God,
who has chosen to treat us always much better than we deserve.

   That is in the abstract. Job's wisdom is conceived in his experience,
before which his heretofore steady belief system is giving way, and
born in a crucible of contradictions and distress. Job, too, wants to
believe that his suffering makes sense, that God does not act capriciously and malevolently toward human beings, and that there is a
way back to relationship with God that will not demand that he per-
jure himself and abandon his integrity. What he knows is that God
has abandoned their relationship for no apparent reason, that instead
of kindness, God continues to treat him as an enemy, that instead of
a parent's watchful, caring eye, God scrutinizes his way of life and

oppresses him with an unrelenting and threatening stare. Job knows, above all, that he is innocent, that he has lived with God and with others as a blameless and upright person, which means receiving correction when appropriate, straightening out his life when necessary, and confessing and making amends when called for. All that he has done. He has done nothing that justifies God's abandonment, torment, and abuse. *That* he knows. And we readers know it too. Remember the opening chapters, with their affirmation by God that "there is no one like my servant, Job, blameless and upright"? And remember how careful he was of his relationship with God that he offered sacrifices on behalf of his children, just in case they had unknowingly sinned? Job's protest of his innocence may make us uncomfortable and even doubtful, but, in the frame of the story, we have God's word for it.

Job opens his response to Zophar (and the overhearing friends) on the same note sounded in Zophar's speech: the issue of wisdom and who is wise. Zophar accused Job of "babbling" and "mocking" God (11:3), and in a derisive proverb undoubtedly intended to be applied to Job, he implied he was empty-headed: "But a stupid person will get understanding, when a wild ass is born human" (11:12). Zophar's wisdom, by contrast, is displayed in his pious appeal to the mystery of God's wisdom, by his presumed ability to see through Job's claims against God, and by his "sage" advice to Job: "If iniquity is in your hand, put it far away" and "Surely then you will lift up your face without blemish; you will be secure, and will not fear" (11:14–15).

Job's retort is equally sharp. Job 12:1 is a difficult verse to translate, but its meaning is clear enough. Job ridicules Zophar's pretense at wisdom, saying, as David Clines proposes, "You are the last of the wise, and wisdom will no doubt die with you" (Clines, 275). As for mocking God, Job protests it is he who is a "laughingstock" to his friends. Zophar has no corner on understanding. Job declares:

> But I have understanding as well as you;
> I am not inferior to you.

> (12:3)

And:

> What you know, I also know;
> I am not inferior to you.

> (13:2)

Job can sing the friends' hymn, acknowledging:

> With God are wisdom and strength;
> he has counsel and understanding.

(12:13)

But Job's wisdom is garnered from his experience and contradicts the neatly packaged version touted by the friends. Job sees the world of his tradition turned upside down. In it robbers are at peace, and those who provoke God are secure (12:6). Job's hymn to celebrate the wisdom and strength of God is a twisted melody that marvels at God's perversity, undermining the institutions of peace, justice, and piety by abandoning and destroying counselors, kings, and priests (12:16–25). Far from offering divine providence, the only wise God seems bent on destruction and chaos. "Look," Job directs his friends, "my eye has seen all this, my ear has heard and understood it" (13:1).

Job's reply to Zophar's claim to wisdom is a counterclaim. Far from being ignorant of the ways of God and life, Job claims his wisdom is in fact superior to that of his friends. On the surface, it may sound to us like two young boys arguing over bragging rights! We would be more convinced, perhaps, by a good dose of humility on either side. But the issue is deeper than that. Wisdom is about what Walter Brueggemann has called a "right reading" of the way things are and about choosing a way of life that is reflective of a deep understanding of the ways of God. Wisdom's word is by its nature debatable. It is not proclaimed with the prophets' pronouncement, "Thus says the Lord." Rather, wisdom depends on sifting imaginatively through evidence from experience, the best advice of trusted friends, and the collected wisdom of the community of faith's traditions to discern truly matters of life and death. Wisdom depends on persuasion in order to tell the truth it perceives, and so it employs all the means of influence at its disposal. Job's claim to wisdom, then, like that of the friends, is really a search for whatever truth may be discerned in the torn fabric of Job's life.

Job and the friends have shared a common reading of the way things are in the world; thus Job can fairly say, "I know what you know." But something radically transforming has happened to Job that has called their shared wisdom into question for him. He "reads" the world now from a dramatically different point of view than his friends, and therein lies his claim to wisdom greater than theirs. He is convinced—he *knows*—that the conventional way of telling the truth that he and his friends have found persuasive in the past cannot make sense of radical suffering, cannot explain how a "blameless and upright" person can be so hopelessly alienated from family, friends, and, most painfully, God. His wisdom is "greater" because he now insists that any right reading of the nature of humankind, creation, and God must make room for understanding cases like his that do not fit the traditional formula that found evidence in suffering and loss of an unrighteous life, justly out of favor with God. The friends, for their part, grant no exception to the rule; instead, they strain to find fault in Job. Job does not have an answer yet, but he has the wisdom and the courage to recognize that the traditional way of reading the world doesn't make sense any more.

In search of understanding, Job returns now to the hope he introduced in chapters 9–10 of taking God to trial in order to force God to justify the suffering that has so crippled him (13:3). In such a trial, Job contends, the friends would prove to be false witnesses, telling lies about Job in order to be on God's side (13:7–8). Fair witnesses do not show partiality toward either side in a legal dispute. In Israel's court process, they were not witnesses for the state or witnesses for the defense, as they are in our system of jurisprudence. Rather, witnesses were expected to testify to the truth in a matter, without showing any favor or partiality, and penalties for bearing false witness were severe (see Deut. 19:16–19). If the friends think they will find favor with God by pleading God's case (13:8), Job warns, they are badly mistaken (13:10). Ironically, they who advise Job that he is in mortal danger if he does not admit to his iniquity are, in their rush to defend God, putting themselves in peril. Job dismisses them as "worthless physicians" and liars.

Turning from the friends, Job presses his case against God, despite having earlier dismissed the idea of a trial of God as impossible, at best, and self-destructive at worst. We can hear the fearful determination in his voice:

> Let me have silence, and I will speak,
>   and let come on me what may.
> I will take my flesh in my teeth
>   and put my life in my hand.
> See, he may kill me; [but] I cannot wait;
>   I will defend my ways to his face.
>
> (13:13–15, my translation)

53

His courage rests on his integrity: "Look here, I have prepared my case; I know that I am innocent" (13:18; my translation). Of God he asks only two concessions in the hope of securing a fair trial: a momentary respite from persecution and dread (13:20–21).

The focus of the trial is set out in two closely related questions for which Job desperately needs answers. Job needs God to name the sins that would justify the devastation Job has experienced (13:23). It is a dangerous, taunting question, since Job is resolutely sure of his innocence. The second question is more poignant, and in it we can hear Job's longing: "Why do you hide your face, and count me as your enemy?" (13:24). "Enemy" is relational language and indicative of what Job really wants to accomplish with the trial. It is not vindication he wants, after all. It is something more, something that goes beyond a legal judgment. Job desperately wants the relationship with God he once enjoyed, when he called on God and God answered, when God let God's face "shine upon him, and be gracious to him, and give him peace," in the words of the benediction we hear often at the close of worship. How far removed from God Job feels is caught up in his self-designation as God's enemy. Once Job believed himself beloved by God; now, for some yet unknown reason, God, Job believes, has turned against him. Divine love has become divine enmity. Trials seldom make friends between enemies, of course, and cannot bring about meaningful reconciliation. One suspects Job knows that too. The futility of Job's longing for a trial with God rests not only in the imbalance of power between the two parties involved but in the impossibility of a judicial proceeding achieving what Job truly wants. Suffering mourns most the loss of relationships. We know that as well as Job does.

> [Job's] cries seem to arise in the depths of our being, and his longing for God who withdraws farther and farther away strikes a familiar chord in us. This means that Job's exemplary character extends to the present, transcending time and space, for his suffering resembles our own. (Crenshaw, 103)

Having placed before God the issues of the trial Job demands, he grows more reflective in his address (chap. 14). His own decaying condition is symptomatic of the whole human condition. Life is fleeting, a limited number of days, yet even this precious time is filled with persistent divine scrutiny and judgment. "Look away from them, and desist," Job pleads, "that they may enjoy at least the rest that even laborers know at the end of the day" (see 14:6). This life is all there is; while even trees may enjoy the hope of new life growing out of a stump, humans die and are no more. Death is final, an unending sleep, from which awakening is no more likely than the heavens disappearing (14:12).

Once Job longed for death (chap. 3), but now death has become his enemy, threatening to end his life—miserable though it may be—before Job's trial can come to fruition and reconciliation with God can happen. "If mortals die, will they live again?" (14:14). That is an impossible dream. Yet for a moment Job allows himself to wonder "What if?" He imagines that death might be a temporary hiding place, outside the reach of God's anger. If that could happen, he would gladly serve his time there, until the right moment, when, once again, God would long for him and call him and he would answer. That is Job's momentary hope, that once more he and God would be on speaking terms, and life would be whole again.

Job's hope is only for a moment; quickly the dream evaporates and the harshness of reality returns (14:18–22). Sturdy and resistant as human hope might be, God, Job grimly contends, finally wears it away and destroys it. God prevails, and human life comes to a hopeless end, without even the chance to celebrate their children's achievements. "They feel only the pain of their own bodies, and mourn only for themselves" (14:22). This is a grim assessment of death's power over life. It is as if Job's impossible, fleeting dream has awakened in him even deeper despair. Job's speech began with spirited castigation of his failing friends and ends in unrelieved mourning for himself and the whole human family. One might expect his words to end here; what else is there to say if hope is hopeless? Yet Job is not through. Hope flickers still within his saddened soul and drives him on. Painful and fleeting as life is, Job cannot, will not, let go of it. Something is changed beyond this speech. Having looked at life in the starkest way imaginable, he is even more resolute in his pursuit of a hearing with God. What, after all, has he to lose, given the irresistible erosion of life, except his integrity? Escaping God's "fencing in" of life and the finality of death may be impossible, but Job can still hope against all odds that God may yet answer him and that, before eternity puts him to sleep, he may yet be at peace with God.

The poet's attention to hope in Job's speech draws our attention there as well. For a tree, there is hope. Though "cut down," a verb frequently used of the destruction of human life as well, a shoot may still grow out of what seems dead. We know the truth of the poet's observation. Some years ago a powerful windstorm that blew through Louisville broke in half a much loved magnolia tree in our yard. Sadly,

I cut the rest of it down as close to the ground as the saw allowed. That, I thought, was the end of our magnolia. But by the next spring a fairly hearty stem had grown beside the old trunk, and that unpretentious sprout now has grown into a tall, albeit spindly, still developing tree. Cut down, clearly, the tree was not sapped of its vitality; it regenerated itself. That is, Job affirms, the nature of trees; that is how God created them. The prophet Isaiah uses a similar image to describe hope for the emergence of a just ruler, a messiah, in Israel: "A shoot shall come out from the stump of Jesse, and a branch shall grow out of his roots" (Isa. 11:1). The early church found in this image a way of talking about the significance of Jesus of Nazareth, whom Christians claim as Messiah. For Isaiah and the church the regenerating tree points to God's determination to create something new yet continuous with what was before. Hope, in this image, rests in God's creative intention. While for Job the emphasis falls on the natural character of the tree, nonetheless the Creator's design for the tree is visible in the new shoots it may put forth.

> The bold charges against God aimed at a single goal: to evoke God's response at any cost. (Crenshaw, 106)

Human beings, the poet observes, are not as fortunate as the trees, and that too is by the Creator's design. We are "cut down" and do not regenerate ourselves. To the succinct question, "If mortals die, will they live again?" the poet expects the answer to be "No." We wish it were not so, the poet admits, and for a moment imagines the possibility of life ending differently. Job must find hope within the joys and sufferings and ambiguities experienced between the boundaries of birth and death. For that reason, if "days are few and full of trouble," hope may be illusive. What hope there is in this bounded life Job finds in God's desire for relationship with God's human creatures. Without God longing for him, without God's caring presence, Job finds life tragic. His experience of God as enemy and persecutor leads logically and emotionally to the drastic conclusion that God has destroyed hope for human beings. To be sure, it is a logic born of deep suffering and alienation, and certainly the friends would not agree.

Yet just as surely, the poet touches truth here. Without relationship with God—without a firm conviction that God cares for us, longs for us, and intends good for us—life is hopeless and hardly worth the trouble it brings. God's silence, coupled with the depth of human suffering Job knows firsthand and sees more widely around him, has shattered his conviction of God's good intentions. He searches for something we all need—namely, congruence between our experience and our convictions, apart from which hope becomes wishful thinking. Suffering cries out for God; without response hope dissipates and dwindles to despair.

The poet of Job does not affirm a doctrine of resurrection; neither does his tradition, at least not yet. That will appear late in Israel's life and grow over time in the closing centuries before the Common Era and the birth of Jesus. It is not eternal life for which Job hopes. He hopes for restoration with God within his lifetime. Resurrection faith speaks to Job's crisis for Christians not because it offers an escape from a need to find our present life hopeful but precisely because it proclaims the reconciliation between God and humankind for which Job so desperately longs. Resurrection is God's "no" to every experience of godforsakenness. Yet we know firsthand experiences of suffering and the feel of God's absence. Those are real to us and can render life hopeless, not because we are faithless but because such experiences contradict the faith we hold dear, thereby intensifying our sense of loss. Once again we are not far from Job, for whom, as for us, an irrefutable memory of God's presence pushes beyond despair toward a stubborn affirmation of the value of living.

? Questions for Reflection

1. As Job contends, experience can sometimes sharply challenge our beliefs. Can you think of times when your experience seemed to run counter to your beliefs or the beliefs of the church?
2. Crisis and loss can make us feel abandoned by God. Have there been such times in your life? What was that like and what did you do about it?
3. The author says, "Suffering mourns most the loss of relationships." What do you think he means by that and, in your experience, have you found it to be true?
4. Job's concern is with the possibility of hope for this life. In what do you find your hope "for the living of these days"?

6 Job 19:1–29

"I Want to See God"

This chapter includes two images very familiar to contemporary Christian readers. The first is the source of a popular expression, widely used to affirm a narrow escape from some confining or threatening situation, sometimes real and serious and other times more playful and whimsical. "I escaped by the skin of my teeth" has its origin in Job 19:20, a very sober context that we will explore in this session. For us it is a positive, celebratory exclamation. But for Job it conveys the opposite feeling, as we shall see.

The passage that rings the loudest for us and bears the deepest significance comes in verses 25–27. We can hardly read them without hearing the triumphant and magnificent music of Handel's *Messiah* sounding on Easter morning: "I know that my Redeemer liveth." Their volume is so loud that these words nearly drown out the rest of the chapter. This declaration of faith has special meaning and significance for Christians, for whom Jesus Christ is "our Redeemer" and the one who came and who will come again to "stand upon the earth." The full impact of these three verses on Christian sensibilities is visible in the King James Version of the Bible, which, in this case, is translating an early Latin version of the Bible called the Vulgate:

> For I know that my Redeemer liveth,
> and that he shall stand at the latter day upon the earth:
> and though after my skin worms destroy this body,
> yet in my flesh shall I see God:
> whom I shall see for myself,
> and mine eyes shall behold, and not another;
> though my reins be consumed within me.

The drama and hope of resurrection "at the latter day" seem irresistibly represented in these verses. Yet we must force ourselves to wait for conclusions about their meaning until we have set them first in their context in this chapter in Job. We will discover that the Hebrew beneath our English versions is complicated and open to a variety of meanings, which is evident in a comparison of several English versions of the Bible. If you are using this book in a study group, take a moment to see how the versions of the Bible represented in your group differ and how they are the same. Any word in Hebrew, as in English, has a range of possible meanings. Translators must decide what the sense of a particular Hebrew word may be and then decide which English word best represents that sense. Translators may differ in their choices both of words and the way the words go together in a verse. That is why English versions vary, each of which likely represents a perfectly possible way of reading the Hebrew text.

In any case, we may assume that whatever meaning we find in verses 25–27 now must first make sense in Job's story overall and in the immediate context of the verses and argument that surround them in chapter 19. That means we must "wait and see," hard as that is for us, until we have explored what Job is saying in the chapter and, on another level, how this chapter fits into the story that the poet of Job is developing.

We may say first the obvious. Job's speech is a response to Bildad's second speech in chapter 18. But, as we have seen all along, Job's responses are always intended not only for the prior speaker but also for all three of the friends. That is evident, for example, in the fact that the "you" of verse 2 is plural in Hebrew. In my part of the country, Job might have said "y'all." But the friends are seldom the only audience intended by Job; God, it is assumed, is also fully aware of what is going on and being said.

Job's opening question to Bildad and the others echoes Bildad's opening challenge to him: "How long will you hunt for words?" (18:2). Job's retort is no less exasperated: "How long will you torment me, and break me in pieces with words?" (19:2). Job's words are in search of ways to convince the friends of his innocence and, therefore, of the injustice he has been constantly suffering in their efforts to find some way to condemn him for *something* he must have done to justify God's violence against him. Job's words appeal to the friends to condemn, as he does, God's destruction of an innocent man.

The friends, on the other hand, denounce, deny, and dig mercilessly at Job's psychic sores, determined to expose a flawed character in Job or, at the least, persuade him to give up his stubborn protest and plead for mercy in the face of overwhelming divine power. The friends, with their words, blame the victim, as we might put it. Most of us were probably taught as children the saying intended to stave off the cruel words of other children: "Sticks and stones may break my bones, but names can never hurt me." Experience, however, may have taught us otherwise. Words are powerful and can be destructive and torturing, cutting deeply and abusively to the core of self-perception. To be accused of something you did not do, to be told that you "brought it on yourself" when it is not true, to be battered by another and told it is your fault exacerbates the pain and frustrates the truth.

> Job spoke better than he knew in his longing for an umpire, a witness. and a redeemer. In the fullness of time one came who had his hand on God, for he was Very God of Very God; and at the same time had his hand on humankind, for he was truly human. In him we hear the voice of Job reechoed, "Why?" and the voice of God, saying, "I am the Alpha and Omega, the first and the last, the beginning and the end." (Rhodes, 206–7)

The friends' avalanche of words accusing Job crushes him; the friends are relentless ("ten times" is not meant to be taken literally but is a whole number suggesting "countless" times), yet they have no shame for their constant harassment of him (the meaning of "wrong" in v. 3). While Job makes use of common lament themes in this chapter, the mood is angry, not conciliatory and certainly not pleading. Verse 4 is no exception. Job does not admit to any error here, and assuredly not one that could justify his treatment at God's hands. The form of the "if" clause in Hebrew indicates Job is speaking contrary to fact: "*If* it were true (which it is not) that I have erred, my error would lodge with me" (my translation). There is no justification for the friends' behavior. Despite apparent evidence to the contrary—suffering being taken as a sure sign of sinful behavior—Job has done no wrong. Rather, it is God's abuse of him that is wrong. It is God who "has put me in the wrong," asserts Job (v. 6). Job uses here the same verb that Bildad used in 8:3, which there has the meaning of "pervert." Bildad asked rhetorically, "Does God pervert justice? Or does the Almighty pervert the right?" Job's accusation in 19:6 would seem to imply an answer to Bildad's question: Yes, God *does* pervert justice, and my case is proof of it.

This crucial accusation against God, that it is he who has perverted justice and is responsible for Job's situation, evokes in Job an extended and graphic description of God's violent attack against him (vv. 7–12), including depriving him of relationships with family and friends (vv. 13–20). Job's indictment of God stretches unrelieved from verses 8 to 11, as the NRSV makes clear at a glance, each verse beginning with "He" (i.e., God) and followed by striking verbs: "walled," "stripped," "taken," "breaks," "uprooted," and "kindled." Job cries for help, but God does not answer; he pleads for justice, but there is none (v. 7). God has lodged a full frontal assault on him; he is like a city under siege, like a prisoner of war, publicly humiliated (vv. 8–12). The disproportionate scale of the divine attack against him is vivid in the ludicrous image of a conquering army laying siege to a tent. In chapter 14, as we saw, a tree was used as a symbol for at least a modicum of hope. Here hope is a tree "uprooted" without any chance for new life (v. 10).

As I write this, the television images of the 2003 bombing of Baghdad are fresh in memory. Military planners promised a campaign against the city of "shock and awe," an overwhelming battering of such power that the terrified city would fall quickly and completely. Some commentators complained that the display of power that actually took place failed to live up to the hype. Nevertheless, the magnitude of missiles and bombs unleashed was dramatic, lighting the dark sky with flashes of concussion and fires bright enough to see the skyline of the city in the deep of night. Living through those nights under the rain of threatening destruction and death, air raid sirens screaming their urgent warning, could only have been terrifying and oppressive for the city's citizens, despite vaunted claims concerning the precision of missiles launched from miles away. Something of this sense of being under attack by an overwhelming power beyond control describes Job's present experience. "Shock and awe" is a good expression of Job's experience, and what is most shocking about it is that, in Job's mind, God is the unjustified aggressor. But Job's depiction is even more poignant. Unlike a quick, concentrated surgical strike that brings a war to a close in a matter of weeks, Job likens God's actions to a siege, a long, suffocating, starving path to defeat and death, with earthen walls built around the besieged city that prevent any possibility of escape.

War images like Job's fill our ways of talking about battling sickness and disease, both physical and mental. Corrupt cells, viruses and infections, or deep depression attack and lay siege to vulnerable bodies and minds. The siege can last a lifetime, debilitating movement, overwhelming defenses, starving its victims of needed nourishment—chemical, emotional, and spiritual—until slowly but surely death comes. Resistance requires all the courage and energy that can be marshaled. Medical professionals, friends, and family are enlisted to battle the enemy and provide support. And there are casualties and "collateral damage" in the form of strained relationships, feelings hurt unintentionally, and financial resources drained. Lost, too, is self-identity; there is the sense of being "beside myself" and suddenly dependent and unsure of the value and meaning of continued living. We know something of Job's experience, though we may name our attacker scientifically or call it "demon" or say it's just the way things are. Yet faithful people in the depth of pain may also dare to accuse God, as Job did, and as many of the psalmists did. It is not faith's last word, as it is not for Job, but only faith holding on to God in the face of ungodly suffering can say it.

From battle imagery, Job turns to a more intimate and, because of that, even more hurtful aspect of the "wrong" God has done him (vv. 13–20). Job has been completely isolated and shunned by the whole social network that ordinarily would surround him and be glad to be in his presence. By treating him as if he were guilty of some deplorable crime, God has assassinated Job's character, making him a pariah in the community that once esteemed him and admired him as a wise and righteous person.

The poet uses twelve different expressions in verses 12–19 to indicate social and kinship relationships that have been destroyed by God's unjust attack on Job, moving from kinfolk (NRSV, "family") and acquaintances at the outer edge of the household (v. 13) to Job's most intimate relationship, his wife (v. 17), and outward again to unknown children on the streets (v. 18). Verse 19 serves as a summary of how estranged Job is from the relationships that have meant the most to him: All those whom he has loved (and who loved him in return) "have turned against me" (the root meaning of "turned" here is "to turn one's back" to someone). It is a picture of utter rejection and social deprivation.

David Clines is helpful and to the point:

> In vv. 13–19 no one raises a hand or weapon or a voice: there is nothing physical, nothing violent. Or is there? Does Job want us to understand that the withholding of affection and esteem is a kind of violence, and does he mean that the principal form in which God's violence presents itself to him is the alienation of [God's] acquaintance and denial of intimacy? (Clines, 445)

We know that withholding affection from a small child can, in extreme cases, result in death, and we certainly consider even lesser degrees of isolation and psychological abandonment abusive. Job's isolation is complete; once close, sustaining relationships are abandoned by his three would-be comforters, his kin, his most intimate family, and, most painfully, by God.

We come now to the familiar but difficult verse 20. Two things may be said at the outset. First, the meaning of the verse should make sense in its context, in this case most immediately verses 13–19, the desertion of Job by his friends and family. Secondly, its poetic structure suggests we may expect a close and complementary relationship between the two halves of the verse. Commentators have noted the strangeness of the images in both parts of the verse. Some have seen in the first half a picture of an emaciated Job, who is all "skin and bones," with the bones poking out through the skin. Images of Jewish survivors of the Holocaust or starved children in sub-Saharan Africa come to mind. But that would mean a sudden shift in context to a focus on Job's wasting away, presumably because of disease, something that has not been a concern in this chapter previously and is not continued beyond this verse. Moreover, the picture the verse offers is not of skin hanging on bones, as one would expect. Instead, peculiarly, bones cling to skin

> Prayers carry words, emotions, questions, requests, affirmations. In contact with God, openness is necessary, far more important than our words or phrases or positions or patterns. However, there is nonverbal praying—moaning and wailing, sighing and begging, stunned silence or holy laughter. All of these are elements in our spiritual linkage with God the great Healer. (Turnage, 82)

and flesh, as if they are not strong enough to support the skin. As Clines suggests, it is an image of complete collapse. Job dissolves into a heap, neither supported by friends or family nor even his own skeletal structure. It is as if his own body has deserted him. He is rotten to the core—not, as our idiom suggests, because of his evil character, but because God has "put [him] in the wrong" (v. 6). It is not Job's physical condition, however, that is the real concern here. Job's collapse is emotional and spiritual. We might say that, loveless and friendless, completely abandoned, he is as far down as he can go, fallen into despair. Those of us who suffer from serious depression know the feeling: utterly alone, without the strength to rise, formless and empty, neither alive nor dead.

The second half of the verse completes this desolate inner portrait. But in what sense? How can Job be said to have "escaped," and what can "by the skin of [his] teeth" mean? First, the Hebrew says "with" rather than "by" the skin of his teeth, suggesting that something was left with which Job "escaped." The expression does not have here the same meaning that it has in its common English use: to escape barely, by the thinnest of margins. The meaning in Job's context is tragic rather than happy: All that is left to him in his isolation is the skin of his teeth. Of course, there is no skin on teeth; to suggest that Job means "gums" is a far stretch. Nor can it be said that Job "escaped"; the burden of previous verses in the chapter points in just the opposite direction. Job has not escaped any of the violence he has described. To "escape with the skin of my teeth" is to be left with nothing at all. There is nothing here to celebrate.

As we have seen, Job longs for God to affirm his innocence and establish once more relationship with him, and to do so in his lifetime. But he has become convinced that vindication will not come before his death. He wishes, therefore, for a permanent record of his declaration of innocence to be carved in rock, something to testify to his integrity when he is no longer alive to make his own case (vv. 23–24). With no one among his intimate friends to speak for him when he can no longer speak for himself, at least he could leave behind an indelible monument to his innocence.

What Job believes and what he desires continue as themes in verses 25–27. It will help us to read these verses carefully and, again, in the context of Job's whole speech. Job believes two things pertinent here: He believes that if he were able to appear with God in court and receive a fair trial, he would be acquitted of any wrongdoing that would justify God's treatment of him as if he were a wicked person. And he believes that it is most likely that he will die without any such opportunity to be cleared by God in a way that would make a difference to him personally and publicly. Job's position is that if there is any justice at all, he will ultimately be vindicated.

Verse 25 and the first part of verse 26 express these two convictions. The familiar translation "redeemer" is not the most helpful translation of the Hebrew word *gōʼel* used here. Many English translations misleadingly capitalize the word, as if it were a title. The word belongs to Israel's legal vocabulary, ordinarily designating a kinsperson empowered to "redeem" or act legally on behalf of another family member, usually to keep the household or family intact (see, for example, Lev. 25:25–34 and 47–54; Ruth 3:12; 4:1–6). Job is clear that he has no such kinsperson to act on his behalf. Moreover, he is not in need of a "redeemer" but of someone to speak for him in court, to act as his "champion" (so Clines translates) or "vindicator" (see the textual note in the NRSV) or perhaps "advocate." Verse 25 points to just such a court scene: "I know that my vindicator lives, that he will rise last [to speak] on earth" (my translation). Job's "vindicator" will have the final word and winning word in the trial with God. In Israel's court system, trials were settled by one of the contestants finally winning the argument; the winner, therefore, was the last one to speak. Job's "vindicator" will offer the final convincing argument that will secure a favorable judgment so that Job's integrity is publicly ("on earth") recognized.

The first half of verse 26 points to the second of Job's beliefs, namely, that he will be vindicated publicly most likely after his death: "after my skin has been stripped off" (my translation). Jewish scribes (Masoretes) placed the equivalent of a period after this clause, so that we read:

> I know that my vindicator lives,
> that he will rise last [to speak] on earth,
> after my skin has been stripped off.

> (vv. 25–26a)

What Job deeply desires he voices in his next thought. Though he believes he may die before his innocence is recognized, what he wants above all is to see God while he is still alive, to have God answer his challenges posed so succinctly in chapter 14 (see the previous session in this book). Unbeknown to him at this point, he will have his hopes realized beyond his imagination before the story is out. But at this point in the poem, coming into the presence of God, seeing God face to face, can only be a fervent desire in the face of a certain death. So Job says:

> But, in my flesh, I want to see God,
> whom I would see myself,
> with my own eyes—not another's.

> (vv. 26b–27b; my translation)

Right now, he is exhausted, drained emotionally and spiritually (v. 27c).

We are left to wonder about Job's vindicator. Who or what is meant? That is not clear. Some have suggested it is God, the only one ultimately capable of vindicating him. But in Job's courtroom drama, God is his opponent, not his advocate. God will need to speak for

God's self in any trial that might take place. Perhaps Job's vindicator is an angelic figure, a counterpart to Job's accuser, the Satan. Any vindicator, after all, must have power enough to represent Job in a divine confrontation, a hope Job has previously dismissed as impossible (9:33). In the end, however, it is the vindicator's role rather than identity that is most important. At this juncture in the story, Job perhaps has no idea who it may be, only that he is innocent and someday will be proved to be so.

The heart of verses 25–27 is Job's passionate desire to see God while he is still alive ("in the flesh"). Once more, he moves beyond the legal issues and the questions of justice to the crux of his crisis: his sense of loss and abandonment in the silence of God. While he grieves the loss of friends and family deeply and abhors the injustice of their behavior toward him, it is finally his loss of relationship with God that is unbearable. In Job's view, vindication is key to the restoration of that relationship, a means to a greater end. For Job to see God, God must make God's self present to Job, must show God's self to Job, rather than "passing him by" (9:11) without a word of explanation or comfort or affirmation. Seeing God represents a complete reversal of Job's present state, in which God is hidden and alien to him. It is a metaphor for understanding and a symbol for insight, and Job is in urgent need of both. "Seeing God," in sum, is a word for salvation. In the end, Job's desire is realized. Job's dramatic words following God's self-disclosure in the whirlwind speeches, in fact, echo verse 27: "I had heard of you by the hearing of the ear, but now my eye sees you" (42:5). Vindication and restoration follow, as we shall see in later sessions.

Want to Know More?

About the redeemer in Job 19:25?
See J. Gerald Janzen, *Job*, Interpretation (Atlanta: John Knox Press, 1985), 134–35 and 140–45.

The poet taps primal feelings for us in this chapter. Job is a person unjustly accused, first by God and subsequently by his whole community, including the most intimate members of his family. (On this motif, see Carol Newsom's insightful reflections in *The New Interpreter's Bible*.) We are appalled by such cases in our own time and partly so, I suspect, because we are ourselves so easily caught up in condemning the person accused long before a trial takes place. Such stories are the stuff of television movies, as we watch horrified by the injustice we see and captivated by the accused's efforts to prove his or her innocence. Justice is not only a matter of due process and right verdicts; there is something even more basic involved than that. Injustice offends our often unarticulated sense that right and wrong are fundamental aspects of the world we inhabit, "self-evident truths," as writers of the American Declaration of Independence called them. How core to our existence justice is to us is demonstrated by our conviction that it is also core to God's character. Thus, Job's suffering of injustice is particularly heinous, since the author of justice is, according to the story, responsible for it. We find that hard to imagine, yet the poet of Job challenges us to do just that, at least for the length of the story.

This chapter also touches us powerfully with its depiction of the agony of loneliness and isolation. That is one of the heaviest burdens of being sick or shunned or ostracized or, sometimes, growing old. The Bible's creation stories make it clear that we were created to live in relationships. "It is not good," God said, "for human being to live alone" (Gen. 2:18, my translation). We have our own stories to tell that describe vividly the cost of losing companionship or interaction with old friends. Job's story tells a truth we know only too well. For the church, for Christians individually, such knowledge is a call for building and sustaining relationships with those hidden in plain sight among us, both in our congregations and in our communities at large.

Finally, we are caught up by Job's fervent desire to "see God." That is a hope, a need, we share with him. We want to know what God is doing in our world, in our lives. We want assurance that we are not bereft of God's presence, that we are not left in this world on our own. We want to know how, in the name of God, to make sense of suffering and evil, which the last century has seen in unprecedented measure. The Christian story tells us to look at the life, death, and resurrection of Jesus Christ if we would see God. And we do. We see in Christ the clearest image of God, we believe, it is possible to see. But that is a seeing we must experience for ourselves, over and over again, in life contexts that often blur our vision and distort what we see. Where in the world do we see God in Christ? Faith affirms that we see God in Christ wherever there is love and justice and a whole creation. But that leaves us with difficult questions about the many places we see where those things are absent. We are close to Job's questions now. How do we see God in Christ in places of hate, injustice, and creation's degradation? That is not so clear. God still has things to tell us, to show us. We want to see God in our lives, with our own eyes too.

? Questions for Reflection

1. Job's angry words, like the complaints of the psalmists, express deep-seated feelings of rage toward God that grow out of experiences of injustice, oppression, and disease. Have you experienced such moments of rage and, if so, how did you or do you express your feelings to God?

2. What happens to us when sickness and suffering lay siege to our lives? What is it like to battle back in response, and what allies do we need to help us? How can we be allies for others?

3. Imagine a time when you felt utterly alone. What was that like? Where was God for you? Who are the lonely people in your congregation, and how can you help them?

4. Job longed to see God face to face. In moments of great absence, where do you look for God and what do you hope to see?

Job's Final Appeal

At the end of chapter 31, the poet writes, "The words of Job are ended." The Hebrew word rendered "ended" is familiar to us from our journey through Job's story. It is a word that means "complete," "perfect," "whole." Elsewhere it has been used to describe Job's innocence and integrity. The biblical writer has cleverly and carefully chosen this word to close these thirty-one chapters of courage, tragedy, debate, anger, protest, and lament—all begun by a divine wager about human motivation for worship.

Now we come to the end of Job's painstaking search for an answer—some response, any response—from his silent, remote, divine adversary. To be sure, there is more to come before the story concludes. Job does speak again, but only a few words and in a far different tone than we have heard since chapter 3. We have not heard from God yet, either, and those who first heard the story may have wondered if they ever will. If you have looked ahead, you know we do. Yet something final happens in Job 29–31, so it is fair to say that the words of Job are complete. It is also fair to say that the words of Job are innocent, as is Job himself—something that God will stipulate in a little while (42:7).

This nineteenth-century painting by Leon Bonnat captures Job's longing for a response from God.

Chapters 29–31 are tightly linked to one another, yet each chapter is complete in itself. They are, if you will, three acts to a single drama. Unlike the other speeches of Job, while they are responsive to things the three friends have said repeatedly, these chapters are not addressed directly to any one of them. Nor are they addressed explicitly to God, with the exception of 30:20–23, which is the first time Job has spoken directly to God since chapter 16. God, of course, is presumed to "overhear" whatever is said. Job's every speech, therefore, including this one, is indirectly directed to God, a fact Job means to take advantage of over and over again. Indeed, with this speech, he intends to *force* a response from God, and we will see how he sets about it as we look at these chapters in detail. Commentator J. Gerald Janzen has concluded (p. 201) that these chapters are a soliloquy like chapter 3, which together would form a frame around the arguments with the friends and appeals to God. He argues that chapters 29–31 offer a strong contrast to chapter 3, suggesting how Job has been transformed over the course of the story.

Job 30:28 suggests yet another possibility, one that I favor. Here Job declares, "I stand up in the assembly and cry for help," which echoes 30:20: "I cry to you and you do not answer me; I stand, and you merely look at me." These verses, together with the prominence of legal language throughout the chapters and especially in chapter 31, suggest that Job's speech belongs in a public assembly, before which he declares his innocence and requests that an indictment be drawn up by his legal adversary, that is, God, and a judge appointed to hear the case (see especially 31:35–37). The setting, then, would be in the city gate, where civil issues are resolved, especially if they cannot be settled privately (see Ruth 4:1–12 for an example). This same public setting, rather like the steps of a courthouse, plays a prominent role in Job's recollections in chapter 29. So we should probably imagine these three chapters continuing the theme of Job's wish for a trial with God to hear what charges God has against him that could justify the abusive treatment he has received at God's hands or be exonerated once and for all, as he believes he must be. As it stands now, God's silence condemns Job, since to all appearances he is being treated as if he were guilty of some serious crime. These chapters represent Job's last-ditch effort to force God to respond to Job's appeals for justice and his longing for God's presence and the restoration of their relationship.

"Out of the depths," as the psalmist puts it, Job remembers what life was like before calamity struck and death swept away his children and his livelihood and sickness and despair racked his body and mind. Chapter 29 looks back to days before sorrow, as Job wistfully longs to return to "the good life" he once enjoyed. Notably, he marks these "days of his prime" (v. 4) first and foremost in terms of the relationship he enjoyed then with God. Then God watched over him to keep and protect him, not like now, when God's "watching" is an oppressive scrutiny, constantly searching to expose any flaw or failure in Job's life (see 7:19; 10:5, 14). Then, rather than blocking his way at every turn (see 19:8), God's face shone upon him and lit his way through dangerous darkness. In those days, Job and his family enjoyed the intimate friendship of God; now God is his enemy (see 13:24), perpetrating violence against him. Then God was with him; now God is nowhere to be found (see 9:11).

All that was good in Job's life flowed from the intimate relationship he enjoyed with God. Job's self-portrait is that of a blessed and happy man who enjoyed the respect and admiration of his community. To be sure, it is the picture of a wealthy person belonging to the privileged class who has the freedom to devote himself to public life. He is the beneficiary of a patriarchal and hierarchical society, sharply divided into "haves" and "have-nots." Frankly, it is a picture we know well, even in the context

> [T]he more firmly you believe in a good, loving, and powerful God, the more vexing does the problem of evil become. . . . If there is no God, the problem ceases to exist as a "problem"; if there is a God, the situation seems intolerable. (Brown 1955, 144)

of the more egalitarian values modern democracies hold (but often do not exhibit). Within the framework of Job's social values, he lives an ideal life, secure enough from want and hardship, and committed to doing his civic and religious duty. Daily he was to be found at the city gate, where young and old alike treated him with deference and listened carefully to what he had to say. As a leading citizen, he served as an arbiter in disputes—the very role he longs someone to play on his behalf in his dispute with God. He settled the cases that came to him justly, taking special care to advocate for the most vulnerable in his society: the poor, the orphan, the widow, the disabled, and the stranger, to whom protection and hospitality was owed. He is an ideal royal figure, and the language here bears similarity to that of the royal psalms, such as Psalm 72. He is clothed with righteousness and crowned with justice (v. 14), and, like a good shepherd—also a royal image—he freed the victims of the unrighteous to whom they had fallen prey (v. 17). His counsel was life giving, falling like the spring rains upon those who listened to his words (v. 23), and he brought joy to whomever the light of his face shone upon (v. 24). He was compassionate as well as just, comforting those who mourned and deserving the loyalty and honor that a king receives from his troops (v. 25).

Strikingly, the virtues recounted in this chapter not only describe an ideal earthly ruler, but they are also attributes of the divine ruler. That is especially clear in Job's reference to "the light of my countenance" or "face" (v. 24), which recalls the familiar benediction:

> May God bless you and watch over you;
> May God's face shine upon you, and be gracious to you;
> May God lift up God's countenance to you, and give you peace.
>
> (Num. 6:24–26; my translation)

Is this a case of extraordinary pride or arrogance on Job's part? It is possible to see it that way. But it is also possible to see here a depiction of a faithful and righteous servant of God living in the image of God, conducting his life in accordance with the best instruction of divine Wisdom. Thus, the intimacy with God, which Job recalled so passionately at the beginning of this chapter, is reflected in Job's relationship with others in his community, especially in his fair and just treatment of those who sought his help and counsel. Memory frequently idealizes, however, so we need not think that Job did not occasionally stumble on his walk in wisdom's way. The degree to which he exhibited a righteous life was unique in his community, as his treatment by his peers attests, but the claim that has everywhere been made for and by Job is given color and illustration in this chapter. This is an "upright" and "blameless" man.

Job's memoir in this chapter prompts questions for us. Looking back on one's life as we grow older is something we all do, usually with a mixture of joy, satisfaction, disappointment, and regret. Particularly when things are going badly in our lives we can remember, as Job did, when life seemed more satisfying or hopeful or enjoyable. We wish life were still like that, that we were like we were before, unscarred and unburdened by intervening events. Job's recollection is more than fond memory, however. It is also a measure of the values Job holds dear. The suffering and abuse that Job has endured has forced him to take stock of himself, to probe his own conscience to discern what a "good life," a life blessed by God, looks like. Trying times, we say, test our mettle. "Integrity" describes our ability to sustain deeply held values through such times and not lose ourselves to their destructive forces.

Job's responses to his self-examination are, in the first place, his, but they are also reflective of the values of his community and times. The story prompts us to ask ourselves about *our* values—what constitutes, for us, a good life—but it does not presume that our responses will be the same as Job's. We need not, for example, indeed, ought not, embrace as positive values social stratification, hierarchical power relationships, or patriarchal dominance. On the other hand, there are things that ring true here and recommend themselves as essential values for right living. Job, for example, grounds his values in his relationship with God. The good life is one that grows from knowing oneself befriended by God, loved by God. If Job's pleasure at being renowned in his community strikes us as prideful, it may raise helpful questions about the contemporary values of self-achievement and celebrity, to which, judging by advertising, we pay so much attention. Job's active concern for justice, especially for the most vulnerable of his society, commends itself to us as people of faith, though we may regret the paternalism Job reflects. Job is a person of power and influence who uses both in behalf of those who have neither. We could wish he might go further and redress the social structures that leave so many in his society so vulnerable in the first place, but that the good life is a life lived as an advocate for powerless and voiceless people and other victims of injustice cannot be doubted. Befriended by God, Job befriends others; loved by God, Job loves his neighbors. What, asks the story, can *you* say for yourself and your community?

If chapter 29 recounts the "good old days," chapter 30 brings the present into sharp relief. The contrast is underscored by repeated use of the introductory phrase "But now" (30:1, 9, 16). The very folks who once held Job in such high regard, who benefited from his counsel and trusted his leadership, now make fun of him and mock him in bawdy, barroom songs. Those who welcomed him and gathered around him, just to stand in his light, now abhor him, keep away from him, and spit at the sight of him (v. 10). The NRSV is not strong enough here: The Hebrew may be read, "They spit in my face." Job's bitter and offensive castigation of these poorest of the poor, whom he calls insultingly, "a senseless, disreputable brood" (lit., "sons of stupid fools" and "no-names," v. 8) contrasts darkly with his touted sympathy for the poor in the previous chapter and earlier in chapter 24. Here is a class-conscious Job at his worst. But the point is made: He is the object of scorn by even the "trash" of society. His once proud name is scratched on bathroom walls. His dignity and honor have been stripped from him, driven away by the onrush of the

terrors of death (v. 15). His days of joy are now endless days of affliction and nights of racking pain and no rest.

God, who was then an intimate friend, *now* is his cruel tormentor
(v. 21). The one who was so close that Job needed only to whisper
now refuses to answer his loud cry for justice (v. 20). Instead of his
advocate, God has become Job's divine violator, binding him tightly
with his own clothing and throwing him into muck and mire, like
the dust and ashes from a dead fire (vv. 18–19). Job's life has become
God's cruel joke: Having raised Job to great heights, now the wind
has become a tornado, crushing him toward death (vv. 22–23). By
contrast, Job showed compassion for those who sought justice from
him, intervening on behalf of the poor, moved by their suffering (vv.
24–25). Eliphaz's early question whether anyone could be more righteous than God (4:17) would seem to
be answered in the comparison here
between Job and God as administrators
of justice: Job appears the more righteous! Unlike God, he did not deny justice to an innocent person.

> Comfort, encouragement, strength, wis-
> dom, serenity, joy, endurance, patience,
> determination—all of these are byproducts
> of prayer, gifts from the One to whom we
> address our prayers. No formula can guar-
> antee specific results. Prayer is its own sat-
> isfaction. (Turnage, 82)

Once Job believed, as the friends still
do, in a moral order guided by retributive justice. A righteous life is a good
life, long and peaceful, leaving behind a
lasting, honored reputation. By contrast, wicked living, a sinful life,
brings evil upon itself, short days full of trouble. Now Job knows better; he lived a righteous life and looked for good, but evil came. Job's
face shined bright enough to light the paths of others, but when he
waited himself for light, he found only darkness and days of gloom
(vv. 26–27). His cry for justice echoes in a wasteland, heard only by
other animals of the wilderness (v. 29). Once he comforted mourn-
ers (29:25); now he sings his own mourning songs (30:31), and this
chapter is surely one of them.

Clearly, while this chapter is intended to describe Job's present reality, contrasted with the verdant memory of the ways things were in
chapter 29, the ultimate and audacious aim is to compare Job's righteous administration of justice with God's failure to show the same
compassion and readiness to hear Job's cause and resolve it that Job
showed to those who "cried" to him for justice in the public square.
This is not a comparison prompted by pride but by desperation. Job
would, in effect, shame God into answering him! The approach Job
uses is something like Abraham's careful argument with God in behalf

of the righteous citizens of Sodom (Gen. 18:22–33). In that story, God's angry intention to destroy the whole city, righteous and wicked alike, without distinction is warily turned aside by Abraham's rhetorical reminder, "Shall not the judge of all the earth do what is just?" until God concedes that for as few as ten righteous citizens judgment against Sodom will be withheld. Job's case is still more complex. Job not only challenges God's willingness to "do what is just," but he accuses God of perpetrating violence against him. More than unjust, Job claims God is cruel, a "tormentor" (v. 21). Job and Abraham tread on very dangerous ground here, as Abraham's cautious approach, gaining concessions from the Almighty little by little, shows. Job is less cautious, though clearly aware of God's incomparable power, a point he has consistently conceded (see 9:19). Unlike Abraham, Job has no time left; urgency is motivation for his audacity.

Job's denouncement of God as cruel and unjust, a judge who fails even in comparison with a righteous human elder, is distressing enough for us. For perhaps most of us, this is hardly an acceptable way to talk about God, let alone *to* God. Indeed, that is true for a considerable portion of what Job has had to say throughout his speeches. Some may be inclined to grant Job the truth of his claims and find relief by setting Job's cruel, despotic God over against a New Testament proclamation of God as love. Yet the church has insisted from very early in its history that there is but one God revealed in the scriptures, not two. Moreover, Israel witnessed to God's loving-kindness and graciousness and passion for justice and love as well as God's anger and judgment as fervently as the early church.

While precedents for much of Job's language of complaint are found in the psalms of lament, Job's concentrated use of it is unique and as troubling to the three friends to whom most of it is addressed (and to earlier readers) as it is to us. We need to remember that Job's speech reflects his agonizing experience, which is particularly painful to him precisely because it contradicts his own convictions about who God is and how God acts. It is not all either he or the story will have to say about God before it is ended. What we hear in Job's speeches is the outpouring of a broken heart and tortured mind, faced with making sense of experiences that make no sense in the framework of Job's long-held understanding of God's response to a blameless and upright life.

If we are honest with ourselves, we must confess that Job is not alone in his cries of protest. His bitter and probing complaint that seeks to force a response from God sometimes finds its equal in tearful, longing, begging cries of people we know traversing their own valleys of deep darkness, certain of their suffering and almost nothing more. I have known that place, as others have. I have whispered Job's words and shouted them into my pillow. Ironically, only faith dares shout at God so loudly and accuse God so boldly. Only faith can feel forsaken by God. And only faith can hope against hope that beyond divine silence there is presence and beyond incomprehensibility, meaning.

We come next to the climax of Job's speech, chapter 31. Job has lamented the loss of his former way of life (chap. 29) and graphically decried his present condition (chap. 30). Now he takes his stand before peers and before God and declares his innocence forcefully one last time. The chapter takes the form of an "oath of clearance," a formal sworn statement of innocence that belongs to the juridical language of ancient Near Eastern societies. When an accused person is unable to settle the matter with the accuser "out of court," and no evidence has been found to corroborate the accusation, a defendant could ask for a public trial before a judge or arbiter, whose decision would be binding on the two parties. Job, as we have seen, has already appealed for such an arbiter to conduct a hearing between himself and God (see 9:33; 19:25). Such a process was often initiated by the defendant making an "oath of clearance," declaring his or her innocence in the face of calamitous self-imposed sanctions. The aim of the oath, then, is twofold: first, to declare publicly one's innocence; second, to force a response from the accuser. Job's oath of clearance really consists of fourteen individual oaths. The full form of the oath may be seen in verses 5–6, 7–8, 9–12, 21–23: "If I have done X, then let Y happen to me." Other oaths in the chapter take an abbreviated form, represented by "If I have done X," with the consequence left unspecified (vv. 16–18; 19–20; etc.).

Job affirms his innocence in matters of sexual relations (vv. 1–12), in his relationship with the poor, the widow, and the orphan (vv. 13–23), in his avoidance of greed (vv. 24–25) and idolatry (vv. 26–28, where the moon and the sun represent deities, to whom Job refused worship by not "blowing a kiss" ritually), and in his relationship with his peers and in his practice of hospitality (vv. 29–34). Job's survey of his behavior goes beyond "keeping the law." He has more than fulfilled reasonable expectations of a good and righteous life, and his declarations have the ring of Jesus' admonition to his disciples to be "more righteous" than others, to sin neither with their eyes nor their hearts, to turn the other cheek to enemies, and to give up a coat to the poor (see Matt. 5–7). Job, for example, adjudicates fairly even when one of his servants brings a complaint against him, recognizing that they share a common humanity as creatures of God (v. 15). He not only does his duty to the poor and the orphan but also makes a long-term, personal commitment to them, "raising the orphan like a father, and guiding him from his mother's womb" (v. 18; my translation). Job has incorporated the covenant with God so that its responsibilities are fully integrated in him, a part of him, body and soul. He has not concealed his transgressions from anyone in his community or from God "as Adam did" (v. 33, reading NRSV "others" as "Adam"). He has nothing to hide.

Job calls one last time for an arbiter or judge, someone to hear his case, if only his divine adversary will at last draw up an indictment (v. 35). In place of his honor, which he wore as a crown before God unfairly stripped it from him (see 19:9), he would wear a crown of false charges, rather like a crown of thorns, and willingly appear before his accuser, ready to give an account of his life (vv. 36–37).

Job closes this final speech with one last declaration of innocence, cast as an oath concerning his relationship to the land. Land and the produce it provides are basic to the well-being of society, and land rights were carefully protected in the ancient Near East. The clearest illustration of the violation of land rights is the story of the theft by Ahab and Jezebel of Naboth's vineyard (1 Kgs. 21:1–29). In the story of Cain and Abel, the land "cries out" for justice because of the spilled blood of Abel (Gen. 4:10). And the land is dramatically altered by the behavior of the first couple as well, described in language very close to that of these verses in Job, with "thorns and thistles" growing up in the land as a consequence of sin (Gen. 3:17–19). The connections between that story and Job's concluding declaration may be intended by the poet, who invokes creation itself as a witness to Job's innocence.

If we protest that no one is that good and that innocent, the writer asks us to keep in mind that at the very beginning God affirmed Job's character as "upright" and "blameless," unlike any other person on earth. That does not mean that Job was faultless or never sinned. It does mean that, within the framework of Israel's religious understanding, Job addressed his sin appropriately, offering sacrifice and seeking forgiveness, which he did on behalf of his children as well (see 1:5). Job does not claim to be innocent in an abstract or theoretical sense. Rather, he claims to have lived as a righteous person, acting wisely and generously and fairly toward others and to have ordered his life in harmony with God's expectations. For that reason he expects, as a matter of justice, the continued fruits of a righteous life. But as we have seen, that is not his experience, leading him to conclude that God has abandoned both him and all justice. The moral order is, for Job, shaken to its core. God has, as Job says, turned cruel. This is finally the greater question, not whether Job is innocent, a fact conceded by the story, but who God is in relationship to his suffering and, for that matter, ours. Job asks, out of his suffering, why God is unjust and cruel, an enemy and adversary, one whom biblical scholar David Blumenthal has called "an abusing God." We are more circumspect and wonder, if we dare, if this is true. We believe it is not; Job must be wrong. But we know of profound suffering and mass murder, of decimating disease and abused and violated children, and we cannot help but wonder where God is in the midst of it all. Job has pushed God hard to speak for God's self. Now Job must wait, and we must wait with him, for God to break the silence of unanswered prayer.

? Questions for Reflection

1. Job's recollection of the good life he lived formerly conveys his values and those of his community. How would you describe a good life? Where, if at all, is your view in tension with the values of our society as reflected in advertising and other media?

2. Job's experience shows us how suffering distorts our past by idealizing it, our present by intensifying its darkness, and our future by challenging its hopefulness. Has this been your experience? How does knowing this help you provide care for suffering friends and family?

3. On page 76, the author says, "Only faith dare shout at God so loudly and accuse God so boldly. Only faith can feel forsaken by God." What do you think this means, and how might it help you care for others or help you pray in times of loss and grief?

4. Job has experienced God as an abusing power who perpetrates violence and betrays trust. As you look around the world, how does Job's characterization of God strike you?

Out of the Whirlwind

At last! God finally breaks the thundering silence that has hung over the book since the opening chapters gave way to Job's anguished, near suicidal outcry of chapter 3. The whole drama has leaned in antici- pation toward this moment, and the poet takes us to it simply: "Then the LORD answered Job out of the whirlwind" (38:1). Job's repeated demand is matched word for word: "Let the Almighty answer me," Job pleaded (31:35). In purposeful parallel, the narrator begins the divine speeches, in which God "answered Job." What God will say, how God will answer will unfold over the two speeches in 38:2–40:2 and 40:7–41:34, each one followed by a brief response from Job (40:3–5 and 42:1–6). The power that God's response to Job has for the story and for us depends on the cumulative affect of both speeches and Job's responses. We will devote this session to the first speech, together with Job's response, and the next session to the second speech and Job's final words. The division is for our convenience only; we have here, in truth, two scenes in a single act, much like the arrangement we saw in the first two chapters.

Though there is a brief prose narrative that follows the speeches from the whirlwind and Job's response, readers may rightly expect that the conclusion to the Job story will be found in God's "answer" to Job. But we should be cautious about prejudging just what that "answer" may be. God is, in these speeches as always, surprising. Job brings to this moment profound questions about God's relationship to him and about God's commitment to justice and a moral order in the universe. He seeks from God not so much an explanation as a jus- tification for what he perceives to be God's treatment of him, for the shattering suffering of an innocent man (see the discussion of Job's "oath of clearance" in the last session). While he probes God's intentions in numerous ways over the course of the dialogues, as we have seen, his questions are focused in the two questions he would set before God in a formal trial, if only God would appear in court:

> Then call, and I will answer;
> or let me speak, and you reply to me.
> How many are my iniquities and my sins?
> Make me know my transgression and my sin.
> Why do you hide your face,
> and count me as your enemy?
>
> (13:22–24)

The two questions are interrelated. Job's view of divine justice perceives God as the enemy of the wicked, who rightly deserve punishment for their sins. And Job's devastated life bears all the marks of just such divine retribution. Yet Job knows himself to be a just and upright person who does not deserve God's enmity. So he asks defiantly for God to declare publicly some crime, some fault that justifies God's treatment of him. What he wants is God's testimony to his innocence, an end to his unwarranted suffering, and his relationship with God restored. That would be justice! If God's question at the beginning of Job's story was about Job ("Have you considered my servant Job? There is no one like him on the earth" [1:7; 2:3]) and Job's motivation for his devotion to God ("Does Job fear God for nothing?" [1:9]), Job's question here is about God's credibility and God's willingness to "do right" (see 8:3).

God's answer to Job, then, comes as a response to Job's pleading for his day in court. It is a meeting he has both longed for and dreaded, aware of the fearful power of God (9:16–20) and without any arbiter to "level the playing field," so to speak, and guarantee a fair trial between two so unequal participants (9:33). God's appearance in a "whirlwind" or "tempest" fills the scene with just such a display of overwhelming force. Natural phenomena such as wind and fire and clouds frequently accompany theophanies (i.e., appearances of God) in the Bible. In particular, the same word translated here as "whirlwind" or "tempest" describes the storm wind that accompanies both the initial heavenly vision of the prophet Ezekiel (Ezek. 4:1) and the call of the prophet Elijah (1 Kgs. 19:11), though in the latter case, unlike Job's experience, God's voice is not in the storm wind but the "sound of fine silence" that follows it. God's appearance is both an aural and visual experience for Job, akin to Moses' encounter with the burning bush (Exod. 3:2–4), though the emphasis falls, as in the case of other theophanies, on the words that follow.

Moreover, the poet tells us carefully that these are the words of Israel's covenanting God, whose identifying name is revealed to Moses in the burning bush passage just mentioned. This sacred name, traditionally unspoken by Jews, is identified in Hebrew by four letters, YHWH, and indicated in many English versions, including the NRSV, by "LORD," in small capital letters. The author of Job has not used this designation for God since the first two chapters, so it is notable that it occurs again here in the divine speeches and in the remainder of the book. The effect literarily is to link closely these concluding chapters with the events that set the whole drama in motion, on the one hand, and the events that lead to Job's restoration after the speeches, on the other.

Theologically, by the use of the divine name the poet connects the appearance of God to Job with the faith traditions of Israel, and Job with the most prominent figures within that tradition to whom God revealed God's self for the sake of Israel's guidance and welfare. By the use of the divine name, the writer claims a place for the story of Job within the covenant traditions that shaped Israel's understanding of God and gave Israel its identity as the people of God. Job's story and the questions it provokes universally,

> The book of Job is the voice of each crying out in the anguish of personal existence: "Why?" But it is also the voice of God answering not the "why" but the person. (Rhodes, 203)

though set within Israel's remote past in the days of its earliest ancestors, with characters bearing non-Israelite names, nevertheless involves Israel's and the church's saving God, YHWH. The "answers" that Job receives are relevant for people at the time of exile and beyond who struggle to reconcile experiences of profound suffering, loss, and godforsakenness with faith's affirmation of God's steadfast love and saving grace.

God's first response to Job is not, as we might have expected, a declaration or explanation that addresses directly Job's indictments and complaints. What God has to say is hardly a "speech" at all. Instead, God confronts Job with a torrent of challenging questions that cascade one poetic image over another, as if to take Job's and the reader's breath away. Indeed, the poetry *is* breathtaking, as if the writer saved his or her best work for God's lines. The content of God's "answer" concerns neither Job's innocence nor his suffering, at least not apparently.

Instead, the theme of the questions is creation or, more particularly, the creative work of God and Job's relationship to it.

In content, the speech is a creation hymn, and shares much in common with Psalm 104, which you may wish to keep before you during this session. In form, it is like Isaiah 40:12–31, in which the prophet, as Israel prepares to return from exile, questions the people about the creative power of God and, by implication, the ability of God to lead them back to the land of promise. The questions in Isaiah are intended to evoke a confession: The answer to "who had done all these things" is "Israel's God alone," who, therefore, is able to deliver Israel from exile. The questions addressed to Job differ from those in Isaiah in that they are direct speech from God and challenge Job personally. Yet clearly the only answer Job can give to God's questions is, as in Isaiah, a confession that God, not he, is responsible for the "wonderful things" revealed in the divine speeches (see 42:3). Job, however, has never questioned God's power in creation, so something more than confession that God is creator of heaven and earth is being asked from Job by these speeches. If, as in the Isaiah speech, the forceful questions that rain on Job are intended to motivate trust, that is a harder project. That will require a radical shift in Job's perception, since, from his point of view, the divine Creator seems bent on destroying the creation (10:8–9). Perhaps the depth to which the change in Job must reach precipitates the power with which the questions come. If so, then the probes God makes of Job have a creative purpose. Their aim is not destruction, as Job feared might be the result of a trial with God, nor humiliation, as some have claimed, but Job's transformation.

God's speech opens with a summons to Job that sets the theme for the entire speech (vv. 2–3). At issue is God's "counsel" or "design" of creation and the depth of Job's knowledge of God's ordering of it. God's characterization of Job's words as "darkening counsel" (NRSV) responds specifically to Job's charge that God's "counsel and understanding" (12:13) has resulted in a dark, destructive reality, such as Job has known. In an ironic statement, Job accuses God of bringing "deep darkness to light" (12:22), not to dispel it but to force human beings to see God's dark design for existence. God reverses Job's charge, accusing him of "obscuring [God's] design" by speaking "without knowledge" (38:2). The Hebrew words for "to know" or "knowledge" and "to understand or discern" and "understanding" occur an extraordinary sixteen times in the course of chapters 38–39. God's indictment of Job is not that he is guilty but that he is ignorant. He has spoken without the wisdom necessary to draw the conclusions he has drawn about God's plan and purpose for creation. Such wisdom belongs, in the first place, to the Designer, who, by wisdom, created all that is (see Prov. 8 and Job 28). "Counsel," "knowledge," and "discernment" are all fundamental words to the vocabulary of Israel's wisdom tradition, to which, as we have seen, the book of Job belongs. By focusing on Job's ignorance, God transforms the courtroom setting of Job's desire into a wisdom school, in which God is the teacher and Job the student. The wisdom Job needs for understanding God's design for creation and, by implication, his place in it, the divine Teacher will provide over the course of this speech and the one following. With fear and trembling Job summoned God the judge, but it is God the wisdom teacher who appears in the tempest (see Habel 1992).

God's questions to Job direct his attention first to the creation and ordering of the cosmos, including the earth, sea, day and night, light and darkness, the primordial depths and underworld, where the gates of death reside, and the stars, the clouds, and the sources for rain, snow, and hail in the heavenly region (38:4–38). The account bears similarities to the creation story of Genesis 1, with its celebration of the formation of earth, dry land, and seas, light, day and night, and a firmament for the stars. There are important differences, however. In the Genesis account, creation is spoken into being by divine command and carefully regulated as a day-by-day

> A Christian doctrine of providence based on the biblical story makes no cheap promises that if we will just trust in God, we will be spared the hardship, pain, and suffering that are the "dark side" of our creaturely existence and the result of the powers of darkness that have invaded God's good creation. (Guthrie, 187)

process, with each day's creation concluded with divine approval of its goodness. In Job, God works not by command but by careful design and construction. God is the divine architect and master builder, who laid the foundations of the earth, after careful measurements, sinking its bases deep, and laying its cornerstone carefully (vv. 4–6). The majestic accomplishment of God's design and construction was dedicated in a service of worship, accompanied by a choir of morning stars and the praises of the heavenly beings (v. 7), the latter being the same designation used for members of the heavenly council that appeared before YHWH in chapters 1 and 2. The joyful music of the heavenly beings contrasts sharply with Job's dark portrayal of God's work as Creator. If the book of Job were composed in the postexilic period, which seems likely, the imagery of God as architect and master builder would have been particularly striking for readers in light of efforts to rebuild the destroyed Jerusalem temple. Some scholars suggest, in fact, that God is depicted here as building a temple. Far from the unholy place that Job described, the earth, in God's design, is a holy precinct, a place for God's dwelling.

God's design for creation includes a proper place and time for everything. The order is careful and complex. The sea is a good example of the balance that is built into all things. This powerful force that threatens constantly to overwhelm the land is a worthy symbol for chaos, and was used as such in ancient Near Eastern creation stories. Job summons those who can "curse the Sea [Heb., *yam*]" and "stir up [the sea monster] Leviathan" in his wish to undo creation and blot out the day of his birth (3:8). He accuses God of guarding him, as if he were the Sea, ready to unleash chaos at any moment (7:12). God's design includes the potentially chaotic sea, to which God is midwife, wrapping it in swaddling cloths when it "gushes forth from the womb" (38:8–9). The sea, like the dawn (v. 12) and light and darkness (vv. 19, 24) has its place, but God has set limits and boundaries beyond which it may not go (vv. 8, 10). God's design is permissive but within appropriate limits: "Thus far shall you come, and no farther, and here shall your proud waves be stopped" (v. 11).

The uncontrollable sea is an ancient image of the magnitude of God's power.

Similarly, light and darkness exist in balance; each with its appropriate time and place. Dawn comes and darkness recedes, and there is a rhythm to life that fits this design. Nighttime belongs to predators in search of their prey, but, as the psalmist says, "When the sun rises, they withdraw and lie down in their dens. People go out to their work and to their labor until the evening" (Ps. 104:22–23). The wicked, too, are people of darkness, who operate under its cover, but when dawn comes it "takes hold of the edges of the earth that the wicked be shaken out of it," like sheets shaken clean in the morning (Job 38:12–15, my translation). Notably, the wicked are not destroyed, but their power—their "uplifted arm"—belongs to the darkness, not the light. Job had accused God of letting the wicked run unchecked, of "giving the earth into their hands" (9:24). But the power of the wicked is, in fact, restrained by the advent of light, not only in the sense that daylight is a safer time to be on the streets, but wickedness and light are incompatible in the moral sense as well.

God's design for creation includes provision for annual seasons, tracked by the movement of the stars, which God guides, though Job cannot (vv. 31–32). Rain and lightning, snow and hail, winter and summer (vv. 22–30) come in due time at God's direction. God nurtures and cares for the earth, and the generosity of God's care is evident in the rainfall that waters even "the waste and desolate land" (lit., "the wasted wasteland") to produce grass in places "where no one lives" (vv. 25–27). This is the place that no one wants, where outcasts are forced to live and scrounge for food—the detested place for detestable people, so vividly described by Job in his bitter denouncement of the riffraff who, in his misery, treated him with contempt (30:1–8). Yet God is in even this desolate place, providing rain for vegetation to grow. What seems a godforsaken place to people is not at all. An important hint is here for Job that God's design encompasses more than human experience and human needs or desires. That point will be made more than once before God's speeches come to an end.

From the cosmic realm, God's attention turns to the animal world (38:39–39:30). The challenging questions to Job continue, each one becoming an occasion for further disclosure of God's design of creation. The menagerie that God passes before Job consists of lions, birds, mountain goats, the wild ass and ox, the ostrich, and the horse. They are all wild animals, with the exception of the war horse, yet there is an untamed quality to this powerful animal as well, as it stamps its feet and strains against the bit, so eager to enter the battle. Missing from the scene entirely is humankind, whose absence is particularly striking, given the elevated role the creation of humans plays in Genesis 1–2. Gerald Janzen has suggested that humankind is present in the divine speeches by virtue of their being addressed to Job. "Humankind," he writes, "is that part of creation whom God addresses with questions concerning the rest of creation. . . . To be a human being is to be a creature who is yet God's addressee and whom God confronts with the rest of creation vocationally" (Janzen, 228–29). The point, then, cannot be that human beings are unimportant to God's design. Rather, God fixes Job's attention—and ours—on "where the wild things are," because it opens up a world in which human beings are not the measure of things, where "worth" does not depend on creatures' usefulness to human beings. Here is the wild ox, who cannot be tamed to the plow (39:9–12), and the wild ass who roams free, unfettered, and laughing at any who would tie it to human bidding (39:5–8). Still, God has given a home to each and provides for each, like a mother finding food for hungry lion cubs or fledgling ravens crowded in a nest (38:39–41). Outside the farmer's calendar, in God's good time, the mountain goats and deer come into season, give birth, and raise their young (39:1–4).

God's design is variegated. For some to live, others must die. There is birth and loss, and barren habitat in which the wild ass roams, and lush wild grass for the wild ox's crib, and carrion for vultures to pick (see v. 27; the word translated "eagle" in the NRSV may also mean "vulture," which fits the image of v. 30 better). Nowhere are the extremes more evident than in the contrast drawn between the ridiculous ostrich and the majestic war horse (39:13–18, 19–25). The foolish ostrich, by God's design, is deprived of common sense enough to protect its eggs or care for its young. (The bird's poor reputation reflects a popular perception, though, in fact, it is undeserved.) Its wings are useless, as the creature itself seems to be. Yet it laughs untamed and defiantly at the bridled horse and its rider. It is a design of paradox and mystery, of beauty and fear, full of life, yet not without suffering. By contrast, the horse is endowed with power, "its neck clothed with thunder" (v. 19; my translation). It is the picture of nobility and courage as it tears across the field, nostrils flared, and chomping at the bit to get into battle.

God's design makes room for all of this diversity, and provides for the welfare of God's creation. The wild creatures, no less than the earth, stars, rain, snow, and hail, are participants in a cosmic dance choreographed and directed by God. Far from the dark reality that Job denounced, God's design is a delight, evoking praise and music from the morning stars and laughter from wild ass and ostrich. It is the work of divine wisdom, a providential plan that permits within limits, grants freedom within boundaries, and nurtures life that lives with death and suffering.

God's first speech ends with a final challenge to Job, this one in language that reminds us that God's appearance to Job is in response to his demand for a trial:

> Will he who brings suit against the Almighty instruct me?
> Will he who arraigns God answer me?
>
> (40:2; my translation)

Job has accused God publicly of acting capriciously and fomenting chaos, of bringing darkness out of light, of being a Creator bent on destroying creation. Job has read reality with lenses darkened by his own apparently unjust treatment at God's hands. God answers Job's charges with questions Job cannot answer; he has neither the experience nor the insight to do so. They are rhetorical questions—a teacher's device—that lay open before Job a stunning description of God's carefully wrought design of creation. Now, at the end, God asks his challenger what he has to say. Can Job add anything or correct anything? What has he now to tell God? The tone is corrective but not mocking. God's rhetoric does not intend to humiliate Job but to force him to examine his own perceptions of reality and, in the process, reconsider his own place in it.

Job's "answer" to God is brief (40:4–5). It consists of an admission, a gesture, and a declaration. The moment invites our imagining just what we would expect him to say. Perhaps he should protest that God is off the subject. The substance of Job's case has not been addressed; there is nothing in God's speech about Job's guilt or innocence. Job's insistent protest of innocence still stands, so perhaps we should expect him to assert his hope for vindication one more time. We might expect some expression of terror before the awesome power of God disclosed in the whirlwind of questions. After all, Job himself expected to be terrified if God should show God's self. But Job's first word is neither of protest nor of terror. It is, rather, a word of humility, an admission of awe, and an expression of wonder: "I am of little worth" (v. 4; my translation). It is a comparative word that embraces the great gap between the creature and the Creator. Job had complained that he could not get a fair trial with God without a mediator to moderate the inequality of power between them (9:33). Yet there is no complaint here, only submission. In his closing words, he had vowed to approach God "like a prince," to give God a full accounting of his life (31:37). But there is no princely purple here, just servant's threads. He has heard what God has to say; who is he to say anything in return? In the presence of God, Job begins to see himself, as well as God.

When Job recalled his former life and his reputation and standing in his community, he took pleasure in remembering the deference shown him, because of his wisdom, by young and old alike. As a sign

Want to Know More?

About God's answer to Job? See Robert McAfee Brown, *The Bible Speaks to You* (Philadelphia: Westminster Press, 1955), 156–65.

About models of God in Job? See Carol A. Newsom, "Job," in *The Women's Bible Commentary*, ed. Carol A. Newsom and Sharon H. Ringe (Louisville, Ky.: Westminster/John Knox Press, 1992), 135–36.

of that deference, "the nobles refrained from talking, and laid their hands on their mouths" (29:9). Job now takes up the same gesture to signal his respect for God and his intention to listen, rather than speak any further. His closing words in this reply confirm the gesture (v. 5). Job has said what he wanted to say; he has made his case repeatedly and has nothing more to add. Now he is prepared to listen respectfully. He will, in fact, speak one more time at the close of God's second speech. But the adversarial tone he has taken with God in God's absence is gone in God's presence. Job has moved from anger and accusation to a self-silenced attentiveness to God's word still to come. The change in him is not the result of threat or condemnation. It is born, instead, from a glimpse of God's complex design of the world Job thought he knew. For Job, the world revolved around a clear principle of right and wrong, with persons rewarded appropriately with blessing or punishment within a retributive system administered by a just God. Job's case against God assumes not that the system is wrong or the principle misunderstood but that God has failed to govern the created order justly. But God's "lesson" to Job describes a world that is more "both/and" than "either/or," a place of contradictions and ambiguities, with times and places for "everything under the heavens," to borrow a line from Ecclesiastes. Job has not yet given up his case, but he has given up arguing it further. He will wait and listen, for now.

? Questions for Reflection

1. What did you imagine God's first words to Job would be?
2. Compare God's description of creation here with Genesis 1:1–2:4a. How are they similar and how are they different? What significance do you see in the comparison?
3. The author suggests this is a celebratory creation hymn. What do you see celebrated in it? What would you include in a hymn of creation if you were writing it? You might try individually or as a group to write a creation psalm, like Psalm 104.
4. What do you think Job has learned from God's first speech? How do you think it has changed him? What have you learned about God and yourself?

9

Out of the Whirlwind a Second Time

God is not yet finished with Job, and with good reason. There is little in Job's response to what God has said so far that suggests a fundamental change in Job's perspective. Job, hand over his mouth, is poised to listen reverently, but his case with God is not yet settled. Patiently yet forcefully, God continues to press Job toward a different understanding of the world and his place in it.

God's second speech begins just like the first, with divine confrontation and demand for answers to questions that test the limits of Job's understanding (40:7). The theme for the speech is set in verse 8: "Would you discredit my justice; would you condemn me, that you may be right?" (my translation). God's question borrows from juridical vocabulary familiar to us now from the dialogue between Job and his friends. Job has indeed questioned God's justice fundamentally. He has accused God, in Bildad's words, of perverting justice (8:3), and of "[taking] away my right" (27:2). "Though I am innocent," Job declares, "I must appeal for my right" (9:15; my translation).

In Job's view, the fact that he is innocent and yet has been treated as if he were guilty (see 10:2, "condemned") can leave no doubt about God's failure to uphold justice. Job's hope for a trial reflects the incredible tension in which he lives and the impossible situation that he confronts: In order to obtain a declaration of innocence ("be right"), God must be declared guilty ("condemned"). The legal framework within which Job sees his experience does not allow for any choices other than guilt or innocence, right or wrong. Still, the frankness of God's question to Job, with its logical yet disturbing conclusion that God must be condemned or declared guilty if Job is innocent, discloses the tragic limitation of Job's perspective and begins to push him toward a larger, more inclusive view of reality. Implicit in this troubling verse is the possibility that the "either/or" Job has set up is not necessary. Verse 8 opens the possibility, up to now unthinkable to Job, that his innocence and God's justice may *both* be affirmed. Job can be innocent and God still be just. What is needed is a larger sense of justice. "Justice" has to do with determining guilt or innocence, to be sure, but in its broader sense it is also concerned with governance (see Newsom 1996, 616). The Hebrew word for "judge" or "ruler" (*shophet*), used to describe the early leaders of Israel (for example, the "judges" of the book of Judges) is a form of the word for "justice" (*mishpat*) that occurs in verse 8. God's second speech is concerned with this kind of justice, with God's governance of creation.

The tempestuous voice that challenges Job implicitly addresses two troublesome questions. The first asks about God. If God is not to be constrained within a human legal and moral system of strict justice that knows only guilt or innocence, punishment or reward, then how does God govern in a just and moral way? The second question is about Job's identity and, by extension, ours. Who is Job, and what is his vocation in light of the revelation of God that is unfolding before him? If Job cannot be defined by guilt or innocence, then who is he in God's creation and how can he make sense of his suffering?

After the introductory verses (40:5–8) at which we have been looking, the remainder of the speech may be divided into three major sections. In the first (40:9–14), God challenges Job's power to assume God's mantle of moral authority. That theme is implicitly continued in the second and third sections, the first of which describes the awesome beast Behemoth (40:15–24), while the final section deals with the terrifying, fire-breathing Leviathan (41:1–34).

> The section that we know as Job 41:1–34 in the English Bible is numbered as Job 40:25–41:26 in the Hebrew Bible. This study book uses the English numbering system.

The passage with which this session is concerned, however, goes beyond God's second speech to include Job's response (42:1–6). These are Job's final words in the book and serve as a fitting, though enigmatic, conclusion to the two speeches from the whirlwind and, in important ways, to the whole book of Job. With Job's response, the poetic section that began in chapter 3 comes to an end, to be followed by a prose epilogue in 42:7–17. The final prose piece will be the focus of the final session of our study of Job. But now we return to the divine speech of 40:6–41:34.

God's first question to Job is about power and, more particularly, about Job's power. Indeed, the twin themes of power and pride pervade the entire second speech (see Newsom 1996, 616–17). The two beasts that are the focus of most of it are powerful creatures without parallel, and the closing note of the depiction of Leviathan, which ends the divine speech, extols it as "king over all the proud beasts" (41:34; my translation). God lures Job to a sharp examination of his own humanity with an invitation to put on the trappings of divine office, if he is able, if he has "an arm like God" and a thunderous voice like God (40:9). God's "arm" and "voice" occur often in the Hebrew Bible as symbols of the power of the divine warrior-king who delivered Israel from enemies (see, for example, Isa. 40:10; 51:5, 9; Exod. 15:16; and especially Ps. 77:15 and 18, where God's delivering arm and thundering voice occur together). If Job can claim these divine attributes, then he is suited to "deck [himself] with majesty and dignity" and "clothe [himself] with glory and splendor" (Job 40:10)—all majestic language suited for the divine ruler.

The language used here also has the meaning on occasion of "pride" and "arrogance" or "haughtiness," underscoring the dangerously thin line between appropriate recognition and conceited pride. "Pride," a popular proverb tells us, "goes before destruction, and a haughty spirit before a fall" (Prov. 16:18). If Job is to rule like God, then he must deal with the proud and the haughty. They are to be humbled and the high and mighty brought low, the prideful wicked pressed down so hard they are pushed to "the world below," literally "the hidden place" (vv. 11–13). If Job has this kind of power, God offers, "even I would praise you, because of the victory your right hand can give you" (v. 14; my translation). Were Job able to so destroy the proud, he would be "like God" and worthy of the kind of praise normally offered God. Of course, he is not. He is human, not divine, and his power is not godlike but appropriate to a human being. That will become increasingly clear to Job and to us as the speech continues.

It is tempting to hear in these verses a condemnation of Job and an implicit accusation that Job has been arrogant in thinking that he could bring his case against God to trial. Something like that charge seems to be the burden of Elihu's chiding of Job for his "empty talk" that goes unheard by God because it has the sound of "the pride of evildoers" (35:12–16). Yet apart from the passage before us, the language of "pride" does not play a prominent role in the book of Job, and nowhere is Job explicitly accused of pride or arrogance by the friends or by God. While we may perceive Job's back talk to God as lacking proper humility and consider his insistence on his innocence and his integrity prideful, the story quite surprisingly does not. On the contrary, his language and his behavior are affirmed by God, who says of Job, in contrast to the three friends, that he has spoken rightly about God (42:7). "The proud" are roundly condemned in God's proposition to Job (40:11–13), yet Job is not.

It is not Job's pride that is at stake here but his understanding of God, of God's governance of creation, and of himself. He has never doubted God's power; indeed, it has been frighteningly real to him. He *and the friends* have assumed that they know the rules by which God's power is exercised and, in that sense, have claimed to know more than they do. Pride is not the issue here; limited knowledge and vision is. God's rhetorical questions, as in the first speech, are intended to force Job to see reality differently. If Job were God, the proud would be crushed and driven to their just "reward." But Job is not God, and the proud still exist and act arrogantly and wickedly, all within the bounds of God's good governance. The wicked have their place and their boundaries, as we learned earlier, but they and the proud are a part of God's creation, existing with God's knowledge and assent. That is news to Job.

God next turns Job's attention to two creatures of mythical proportions, Behemoth and Leviathan. The identity of these two beasts has been the subject of much debate. Some argue that while they may be poetically overdrawn, the two animals are identifiable in the wild, on the pattern of the wild animals recalled in the first divine speech. In this argument, Behemoth is a hippopotamus or perhaps a water buffalo and Leviathan a crocodile, both animals hunted in the ancient world. Other scholars have argued that the two suggest mythic beasts, familiar from ancient Mesopotamian epics as monstrous forces with whom the gods do battle. For example, in texts from ancient Ugarit, Baal, the storm god, is credited with slaying Lotan (Leviathan), described as a serpent with seven heads. In Israel's literature, God slays Leviathan at the time of creation (Ps. 74:13–14), and the prophet Isaiah describes the future day of Israel's deliverance as an occasion when God "with his cruel and great and strong sword will punish Leviathan the fleeing serpent, Leviathan the twisting serpent, and [God] will kill the dragon that is in the sea" (Isa. 27:1).

The whirlwind speech in Job, however, does not concern God's defeat or destruction of mythic monsters, as we shall see. Without having to choose between the two opinions outlined, what we can say is that the description of the two beasts paints them as creatures without parallel, the ultimate wild and frightening *others* who lived at the edge of the known world, as Carol Newsom suggests (1996, 215), beyond which, as medieval mapmakers warned, "there be dragons." In our context, in light of verses 9–14, they are further examples of "the proud," whom Job is challenged to humble.

Behemoth, whose name is the plural form of "beasts" (see Ps. 8:8), is a powerful, invincible creature, sturdy and imposing. It eats grass "like an ox" and, far from aggressive, roams the mountains foraging with other animals and cools itself under the lotus plant in the marshy grasslands. It shares features perhaps more with the water buffalo that inhabited the region than the hippopotamus native to Egypt. Striking in our passage is God's opening announcement to Job that Behemoth was created by God "just like you." Behemoth, for all its imposing features, is God's creature, no more and no less. As such, it is the object of God's care as all the wild animals are and has a place in God's order of things—boundaries within which it may dwell, free to roam and yet restrained. Behemoth, like Job, has a proper place within God's ecology. It is a potentially important comparison for Job because it sets him within a vast creation that encompasses a magnificent

> We do live in a dark world. But there is a light shining in the darkness, and the darkness will not be able to overcome it. How do we know? Because even in the darkest days and years we remember the God from whom we come; therefore hope in the God toward whom we go; and therefore, despite everything, can recognize and serve the God who goes with us on our way. (Guthrie, 190)

creature like Behemoth, whom the poet calls "the first of the great acts of God" (Job 40:19), as well as the "birds of the air and the fish of the sea" (Ps. 8:8), the stars of the sky, darkness and dawn, and humankind. Job's world of vision has been far narrower than that, locked on his own suffering and his claims against God, closed in a courtroom, so to speak. He is invited here to see his life on a larger horizon, one in which creatures exist whom God has made, who live beyond human power and control (see Job 40:24). Behemoth is, of course, not just another creature. Behemoth is representative of chaotic elements that are a part of our reality, forces that swirl beyond our capacity to control them. They are part of God's created order, something for which Job's tightly ordered world of "either/or" has had no room.

The foolhardiness of Job thinking he could catch and hold Behemoth (40:24) is carried over by the hunting motif to Job's forced encounter with Leviathan (41:1). What follows is an extended description of a beast far more frightening and ready to do battle than

Behemoth. How far beyond Job's control—and human control, more generally—this dragonlike figure is becomes clear from the detailed description of how utterly removed from human purpose and resource Leviathan is. God veritably mocks Job's impotence to control the creature. He can neither capture it nor domesticate it. Nor will it serve as his plaything or a source of food, flayed and sold in the marketplace (41:2–7). Contrast these impossibilities for Job with the testimony of Psalm 74 or Isaiah 27, which proclaim God's complete domination of this great sea creature, or Psalm 104:26, which celebrates God's creation of the sea and of Leviathan to play in it. Leviathan is a force to do battle with, covered with a double coat of chain mail, armed with rows of terrifying teeth, and breathing fire and smoke (Job 41:12–21). The poet paints a moving picture, as the huge Leviathan, neck bent, without fear or feeling, raises itself to its full height, deflecting as so many annoyances javelins, clubs, or spears hurled against its outstretched body, then crashing down with crushing force so that the sea boils with its rage and foams in its wake (41:22–32). No one is fierce enough to dare rouse this giant (41:10), whose primordial power Job himself enlisted in his bid to undo creation and obliterate the day of his birth (3:8).

The depiction of Leviathan ends with an awesome conclusion that closes the entire whirlwind speech as well:

> Nothing on earth can rule it,
>   a creature without fear.
> It looks down on all the heights,
>   It rules over all the proud beasts.
>
> (41:33–34; my translation)

Leviathan, like Behemoth, is another proud creature that Job clearly cannot humble or bring down. With a touch of irony, the one invited to assume the ruler's role at the outset now, at the end, comes face to face with the sovereign of proud beasts. Governance and power and pride are all mingled here, bringing together themes we have seen throughout the whirlwind speech. For all its mythic proportions, Leviathan is still a creature formed by God and governed by God. The threatening force of chaos, which Leviathan symbolizes, lies uneasily within creation. Yet there it dwells, permitted its power and space but never out of God's control. Like the proud sea, with which Leviathan is closely associated, its waves come just so far and no farther (see 38:8–11). And Job is left to stare, overwhelmed by what he has been shown. As Carol Newsom writes (1996, 631), Leviathan is the "very

94

image of dread (3:25) from which Job has sought escape. When Job confronts it in Leviathan, it is as if a spell is broken. Job is released from his obsession with justice and can begin the process of living beyond tragedy." The divine word comes to a sudden end, without a concluding word of summary or closure. All at once, the stage is left to Job.

How can Job respond to all he has heard and seen? God waits. We wait and wonder. To be sure, the sound and fury that have filled the space for so long apparently empty of God's presence has been stunning and breathtaking, as Rudolf Otto said of the holy, both fascinating and terrifying. Yet the creation panorama with which God has so vividly surrounded Job has meant to move Job to a different way of seeing more than it has meant to satisfy Job's angry, anguished questions. The whirlwind speeches function something like the parables of Jesus—also a way of teaching wisdom—refusing to answer questions directly, preferring instead to shift the ground of conversation to stir the hearer's imagination and capacity to see a familiar world in unanticipated ways. What does Job see now that the divine Teacher has finished the lesson?

Job's response consists of six short verses (42:1–6). Their brevity belies their complexity and ambiguity. Multiple translations are possible, and the NRSV offers one of them. The crux is in verse 6, which has traditionally been rendered, as in the NRSV, as a statement of contrition and submission by Job: "therefore I despise myself, and repent in dust and ashes." But of what does Job "repent"? What sin has he committed? It has been established throughout the book that Job is "blameless and upright," and the voice from the whirlwind says nothing to contradict that. Moreover, if Job repents, then the friends, who have urged repeatedly that he do so, are apparently justified. But the events that follow this scene contradict that, as the friends are accused by God of not speaking rightly and ordered to seek absolution through Job (42:7–9)! Finally, the traditional translation requires supplying "myself" in the phrase "I despise myself" since it is not in the Hebrew text, and it requires reading the final phrase, which literally is "*on account of* [Heb., *'al*] dust and ashes," as "*in* [Heb., *bᵉ*] dust and ashes."

An alternative—and I think preferable—translation of verse 6, suggested by a number of scholars, would avoid these difficulties: "therefore I retract [my words] and have changed my mind, concerning dust and ashes [i.e., the human condition]." In this case, Job makes no confession of sin but recognizes that his case against God has no merit and is inappropriate in light of what he has seen and heard. So Job withdraws it or takes it back, another meaning of the word traditionally translated "despise." He has come face-to-face with God and now sees himself and what it means to be human differently.

We have heard Job on several occasions decry the lot of being human (see, for example, 7:17–18 and 14:1–12), whose days are few and full of pain and suffering, often at the hand of God and always under the aggressively watchful eye of God. Job began his speeches with an agonizing denouncement of his own life, wishing he had not even been conceived. He lamented repeatedly his sense of betrayal, abuse, and abandonment by God, longing for death and a release from a life without relationship to God or family or friends. But now, having seen God with his own eyes (42:5), he has changed his mind, a different meaning to the word traditionally translated "repent." The pairing "dust and ashes" occurs just two other places in the Hebrew Bible: Job 30:19 and Genesis 18:27. In the first instance, the context suggests Job is comparing himself with "dust and ashes" that are thrown out on the ground as trash to be trampled under foot—a vivid depiction of a worthless human life. The Genesis occurrence is in the Abraham story, in the context of Abraham's pleading with God on behalf of Sodom. There it is an expression of Abraham's humility in the presence of God: "I who am but dust and ashes," that is, human. What Job has changed his mind about is "dust and ashes," that is, the human condition, what it means to be human.

> Without even trying to explain why it invades our lives when, where, and how it does, we can remind ourselves and others of the light that shines in the darkness: the light of a loving God who understands and shares the depths of our suffering and dying; the light of a powerful God whose will for our good will not be defeated, who is stronger than death itself, who makes the dead live again. (Guthrie, 173)

Job has finally received what he so desperately hoped for. More than hearing about God, he has seen God (see 19:26), and it has changed the way he sees himself and the world around him. What God has shown Job is a wondrous creation, full of things "too wonderful for me," beyond his knowledge or understanding (42:3). The creation Job has seen is providentially cared for, a place of delight for wild animals who are fed and nourished in even the most remote, humanly uninhabitable places. It is a place of freedom within limits, with a place and time for, as the writer of Ecclesiastes would say, "every purpose under heaven." It is a universe that Job is not the center of, yet he and human beings more generally have a place in it, with freedom and limits. And human beings and Job may rightly suppose that they too are cared for by a generous Creator. The creation Job is shown is not without suffering: Wild lions hunt their prey, and vultures provide carrion for their young. Nor is it without evil: The wicked roam the streets at night, stealing and deceiving until dawn, but their time is strictly limited and their reach contained by a justly governing Creator. What Job could not imagine he has seen with his own eyes: a multicolored world with blended shades of life and death, suffering and laughter, fear and confidence, where even chaos and forces beyond human control have a place within the governance (*mishpat*) or justice of God.

Job's case against God was based on limited knowledge and perception that forced God into a legal system of human construction and reduced suffering to a scheme of moral cause and effect, rendering reality intolerable in the face of human experience. Job now sees things in the light of God's ecology in which human life can be celebrated in realistic recognition of its possibilities and limitations. Justice has a larger meaning, embracing multiple relationships and a complex moral order in which God "makes God's sun rise on the evil and on the good, and sends rain on the righteous and on the unrighteous" (Matt. 5:45 alt.). There is no general explanation for suffering here and certainly not that it is always punishment or a sign of guilt or fault. There is only the recognition that it is part of creation and hence of human existence but certainly not the whole of it. So Job has changed his mind and dropped his suit because he has no longer any charge against God and because he now has what he so long dreaded losing: relationship with God.

Of course, a different reading of Job's closing words would lead to other and different conclusions. The poet has not left us with unambiguous answers, and numerous questions Job and we have raised along the way remain unsatisfied. Numerous interpreters affirm that the author has intentionally left the ending to the reader to complete, thereby inviting us into the dialogue just now ended. I think that is right and a part of what makes the book frustrating and intriguing at the same time. We have more work to do.

? Questions for Reflection

1. Job's claims to know so surely God's rules for governance leads to God's challenge to him that, if he knows the part so well, he "play God." How do we "don the robes of majesty" and "play God" in our lives?

2. Where are the "chaos" places in your life and the life of our world? What do the whirlwind speeches suggest God has to do with them?

3. Carol Newsom maintains that confronting what Job dreads the most releases him from his obsession with it, allowing him to move beyond tragedy. What does she mean by that, and how is it helpful to you?

4. How does Job's transformed understanding of creation and his place in it help you shape your own understanding of God, the world we live in, and yourself?

The Afterword

Endings are critically important in stories, whether in literature or the movies. They are often "make or break" moments that can bring a good story to a satisfying conclusion or ruin hard-won engagement—that sense of really being "into" a story—with an ending that doesn't fit or is implausible or trivializes the depth and pathos of the drama. We expect tragedies to end as Shakespeare's *Hamlet* or *Macbeth* do, with a sense of loss, with issues unresolved and questions lingering. Clint Eastwood's film *Mystic River* provides a more recent example. The story is born in the tragedy of a young boy, stolen from his neighborhood and his youth by a vicious act of sexual abuse, made all the more powerful because it remains a terrible secret that only the audience knows and then only implicitly. Now grown, still living in the neighborhood, his life contorted by unresolved pain, David's path intersects with that of a boyhood friend whose daughter is murdered. David is ultimately blamed for the murder and executed by the victim's grieving and enraged father, who learns almost immediately that he has killed an innocent man. The story ends without justice. The murdering father is left to a life of deception and fear, and David is entombed in the river without an advocate—a death without meaning. It is a hard but appropriate ending, so full of pathos that my mind and heart longed for something more just, while the credits defiantly rolled up the screen.

With a comedy or romance, on the other hand, we anticipate a happy, satisfying ending that pulls all the pieces together and leaves us wishing life were really like that. Television is bloated with sit-coms that end with just such clear resolutions. A story, of course, need not end with laughter to be comedic, but there must be resolution, such as a life well lived or a destination reached. Mitch Albom's wonderful little book *Tuesdays with Morrie* is a good illustration. It is a story of what one of my colleagues calls "dying well," and ends with Morrie's peaceful death and the author's affirmation of Morrie's life as a teacher who transformed a lingering death into an occasion for learning about life. It is a fitting ending to a gentle story that unfolds at the bedside of a wise man making the journey every one of us must make.

What then of the ending of Job? What kind of closure do these last ten verses provide? At first blush, the answer seems clear enough. In the span of these few verses, Job is vindicated, his three friends (Elihu is not included) condemned and forgiven, Job's fortune restored twice over,

Life often gives us reasons to ponder the meaning of our experiences.

his family reconstituted, and his life extended by one hundred and forty years, until he finally dies, after a long and satisfying life. It is the happiest of endings, one of fairy tale proportions: Job lives happily ever after. Tragedy becomes comedy; it is not the ending we expected. Had the story ended with Job's confession (42:1–6), we could have left the theatre pondering the human vocation in an ambiguous world created by a caring God but with profound questions about justice, suffering, and a moral order still unanswered. Job's encounter with God was transforming. His case against God was demanded by a perspective that divided reality into innocence or guilt and confined God's justice to reward or punishment accordingly. What Job sees in God at the end of the whirlwind speeches is a reality far more complex and ambiguous, a Creator with a far more complicated role to play as designer and governor than a doctrine of retributive justice allows. In the world God shows Job, there is a place for innocent suffering, so Job's litigation against God is moot, and he withdraws it.

Job's new view of God and God's world requires him to rethink the human vocation as well. At the very least it requires that human beings learn to live in the richly textured reality that God has created, with all its ambiguities. That is a more difficult calling than finding your way in a reality neatly divided between good and bad, reward and punishment. Wisdom, in Job's new world, requires human beings to live with a kind of ignorant knowledge—a wisdom that knows its limits while embracing its possibilities. Human beings live, Job has discovered, in a world laced with mystery, a world of ordered chaos in which we have a place and a role to play but not the only one. Job's confession brings us this far, with loose threads hanging all about. If the book ends at 42:6, the ending is meaningful but not tidy. Still it seems fitting, if living with ambiguity is inherent in human being, that the book should end ambiguously—art, in the end, imitating life.

In fact, we have a different ending—a "happily ever after" ending that nevertheless leaves pressing questions still unanswered. Indeed, the concluding ten verses raise questions of their own. To begin with, why does the style of the writing turn suddenly from the poetic form we have been following since chapter 3 to prose, the style of chapters 1 and 2? The change in style, coupled with close connections in content between 42:7–17 and especially chapter 1, leads some commentators to conclude that these last few verses provided the ending to an ancient tale still visible in chapters 1–2 about a righteous sufferer named Job. In this old tale, it is argued, the hero Job remained steadfast and faithful despite his suffering and, in the end, God rewarded his loyalty generously, as these concluding verses contend. The author of Job, the argument continues, used fragments from the old tale to begin and conclude his own story of Job, replacing a hypothesized earlier middle part that portrayed Job successfully rebuffing temptations of family and friends alike to "curse God and die" with his own dialogues between three friends and Job. In the present "revised" middle version, however, the friends are the ones who seem steadfastly defenders of God, while Job's aggressive argument with God borders on the blasphemous.

In the present shape of the story, the "old" ending seems strikingly out of place, yet the author of Job has consciously crafted the conclusion as we have it for, we may presume, some good reason. Even if, as other commentators do, one concludes that the author of Job is responsible for creating chapters 1–2 and 42:7–17 from new cloth, the unexpected character of the ending has a startling effect, as the author must have intended. Why it "fits" so uneasily into its present place will become clearer if we tend to a few other questions that it raises.

If the prose form is a shock, more shocking still is the divine condemnation of Eliphaz and the other two friends and the affirmation of what Job has been saying. God accuses the friends—and the personal name of Israel's God is used here as it is in the opening chapters—of not speaking about God "correctly" (Heb., *nekona*; NRSV, "what is right") "as my servant Job has" (v. 7 and again in v. 8). If the Hebrew word meant "passionately" or "sensitively" we could see readily how it could describe Job, though it would seem apropos of the friends too. Instead, the word means "to be right, to have the facts straight" (see 1 Sam. 23:23, where the NRSV translates "sure information"), or "to speak the truth" (see Ps. 5:9). Yet the abundant restoration of Job, if he would only turn to God and repent, is just what Eliphaz and Zophar claimed would happen (5:17–27; 11:13–20), so it would seem that *they* were correct about God. Indeed, the author's comment that Job's latter days were blessed more than his former days (v. 12) echoes Bildad's promise in 8:3. It is harder to see in what sense Job may be said to have spoken about God correctly, especially in light of his own admission that he didn't know what he was talking about (see 42:3; 38:2). So how are we to make sense of God's vindication of Job's loud protests against God and his accusations of God's persecution and tormenting, his abandonment and betrayal of Job? We will come back to this troublesome question.

> Mystery—reality beyond our understanding—shapes our spirituality, our connection with God. An evidence of this mystery is the human companionship that fires up our spirits. In other words, people with whom we are bonded are often gifts from God. Another dimension of this mystery is the fact that God chooses to be intimately connected with people who are hurting or damaged, who are being healed. (Turnage, 82)

There is still another troubling feature about this present ending. It seems to minimize the profound struggle with God and the gnawing experience of suffering that characterize chapters 3–31. It is as if the rosy restoration justifies the awful existence Job has endured, as if the divine voice had said, "Never mind what's happened to you; it's all better now; in fact, you're better off than you were before." If we who suffer with no one to blame, not even ourselves, have been able to see and feel our anger, frustration, confusion, isolation, occasional hopelessness, and sometimes deep despair in Job's words, if Job has given voice to our sometimes speechless feelings, this ending is bitter and offensive. Our healing, if it comes at all, is often, perhaps most often, far slower, far more deeply scarred, and far less enriching than the present ending of Job's story represents. For many of us, the best we hope for is the ability to cope with our daily reality with the support of friends and family and to experience God's love in their kindness and our shared "rage against the night," as one poet put it. Those who suffer know what the present ending seems to ignore: Whatever the future, it cannot go unqualified by the pain of past and present. There is a hint of recognition of this reality in the sympathy and comfort shown Job by family and friends (v. 11). Still, it is a modest word in the wake of the flood of tears that wash over the book.

Why then has the author provided his profound, searingly honest, and carefully crafted work with an ending that seems so misfit and so unexpected in light of the powerful words of Job's lament (chap. 3), the acrimony of the dialogues, the majesty of the whirlwind speeches, and the awakening of Job in 42:1–6? Is the purpose to trouble the waters for the reader one more time, with an ironic twist that throws open the ending rather than closing it, stirring up more questions rather than wrapping things up? That is a start. To say that the ending creates intentional "dissonance" (Carol Newsom's word) with the poetry that precedes it is important, not least because, as every good teacher knows, dissonance can be creative and introducing it is critical to learning something new. And we who are readers of Job are students of a wise teacher.

Unmistakably, Job 42:7–17 takes us back to the beginning in chapters 1–2. The mention of the three friends by name takes us there, as well as connecting to the dialogues. So too does the use of "YHWH" (NRSV, "the LORD"), the sacred name of Israel's God, used prominently in the book in the first two chapters. Job's sin offering on behalf of the friends "who did not speak the truth" about God is reminiscent of his offerings in behalf of any sins his children may have committed unknowingly (1:5). Job's possessions are restored precisely double the number of livestock mentioned in 1:3, and he is once again the father of seven sons and three daughters, the exact count of 1:2. Job had accused his wife of being foolish in her admonition that he curse God and die, rather than cling to his integrity (2:9–10), while 42:8 describes God's threat to punish the friends as treating them with folly (NRSV, "to deal with you according to your folly" transfers "folly" to the friends, while the Hebrew text clearly names "folly" as the way God will treat them apart from Job's intercession). Missing from the closing verses are Elihu, the fourth friend, who does not appear in the opening chapters either, and the Satan, who is absent because he has served his purpose in the story as provocateur. Finally, God's close relationship with Job, articulated in the title "my servant Job" (1:8; 2:3) is affirmed by the same designation in 42:7–8. And though the vocabulary of 1:10 is not used, Job is once more "hedged in" with blessings, possessions, and family in 42:10–17.

Things have changed, however. The events of 42:7–17 take place after, as Job's family and friends put it, "all the evil that YHWH had brought upon him" (42:11). In that light, things look different. As we have seen, Job has changed his mind. Having seen God, he knows what he did not know before: God's governance—God's justice—is more inclusive and complex than courtroom analogies allow for. God is no judge confined to mandatory sentencing. At heart God is creator rather than adjudicator, and even the wicked have a limited place in the scheme of things for reasons God only knows. Justice, it seems, includes even care for the unrighteous. Creation includes restrained chaos and undeserved death, along with green pastures and seasons of growth. Divine wisdom creates and nurtures and summons human beings to awe and a life of reverence and responsibility as creatures made in the image of God.

Still, lest we forget, the anger of God, poised at the friends, is a reminder of human accountability for our words and actions. That God's way cannot be neatly defined by a closed system of reward and punishment does not mean that ethics do not matter or that God does not know right from wrong. The friends are held accountable for not speaking rightly about God and threatened with judgment vaguely described as God treating them foolishly (v. 8), perhaps with the sense of exposing them to shame or disgrace, as some commentators have suggested. If the punishment fits the crime, whatever its precise meaning, the strange use of "folly" to describe God's action suggests that the hapless friends' "not right" speech about God was the speech of fools, like the words of Job's wife urging him to "curse God and die." Is judgment retributive, after all, as the friends suggested all along?

On the contrary, God chooses to provide a means of reconciliation. The friends' sin offering and, above all, Job's prayer persuade God to set aside judgment. Justice is tempered with mercy, and it is worth noting that God initiates the means toward reconciliation— mercy motivated by love. Forgiving the friends is an act of divine freedom and grace. The friends were right: God does forgive and restoration can follow repentance. But repentance does not *compel* God to forgive or restore. Grace cannot be manipulated. Indeed, grace need not even be asked for. God offers it even before repentance, as God's initiative toward the foolish friends suggests. Justice is guided, then, not by a retributive principle but by a grace-full God acting in freedom.

In the opening chapters, God sang the praises of "my servant Job" which, ironically, very nearly cost Job his life. God described him as "blameless and upright," a person who "feared God and turned away from evil"—the very opposite of the "fool." These attributes are precisely those in question across the chapters between the beginning and the present ending. The Satan predicted they would all fall away once Job's steady life was touched by disorienting loss and pain and suffering. "He will curse you to your face," the Satan said (1:11). Beyond chapter 2 God has nothing more to say about Job or to Job until the speeches from the whirlwind, and there Job is blown away, berated, and his terribly limited knowledge of God's creation and justice compellingly exposed. As a result, as we have noted, Job's perspective is changed dramatically, though the long speech detailing Job's changed views that we might hope for from the author of the story never comes. Now, at the end, God once more speaks about Job, though this time not *to* Job. And, once more, it is with approval, though now the words are

> [T]here are many instances where suffering has deepened the compassion and understanding of those who have endured it. (Brown 1955, 151)

about someone whose pain we have felt, whose rage we have heard, whose tears we have shared, whose tenacious integrity we have admired, and whose desperate longing for divine approval we have joined.

We want a speech "in defense of Job," but we get two indirect asides. First, in God's speech to Eliphaz, Job's speech about God is contrasted with that of the friends, who "have not spoken of me what is right [*nekona*], as my servant Job has done" (vv. 7–8). Secondly, God directs Eliphaz and the friends to Job for the offering and intercession they need for their own forgiveness. The irony here is delicious and important. It was Eliphaz who, urging Job to repent, promised that, were he to do so, he would be embraced by God so that "he will deliver even those who are guilty; they will escape because of the cleanness of your hands" (22:30). Eliphaz was more insightful than he knew. The narrator affirms that God "accepted Job's prayer" for the friends' forgiveness (42:9), something Eliphaz never imagined needing.

If Eliphaz is correct about Job's intercessory power, born out of God's favor toward him, he is also correct about the "cleanness" of Job's hands (22:30). Job remains at the end "blameless and upright," his integrity intact. He has steadfastly "feared God and turned aside from evil," though his speeches accused and questioned God relentlessly, with full-throated protests against innocent suffering and divine silence. Job's commitment to God was not something he held lightly and passively but something to clutch after and shake and rattle and make demands with but always without letting go.

In the play *Angels in America* the lead character, a victim of AIDS, in a fever-pitched hallucination sees himself grab hold of an angel, who in her desperate, screaming, flailing effort to shake him loose, pulls him from his hospital bed, toward the heavens, bursting through the walls and ceiling of the room. Yet he will not let go until the angel blesses him. He is caught in his struggle between heaven and hell, but he will not let go, because to do so would cost him his life and he is not ready, despite the suffering, to end it yet. He demands, instead, a blessing and more life, even if it is life with AIDS and only lasts a little while. "I want more," he says, knowing "more" may be without things getting any better and, quite likely, with more pain to come, more sickness. Still, he clings to life and to the angel and to hope.

This scene catches something of Job's relationship to God as well: a screaming, clinging, struggling, protest against death and dying, in search of "more" and a blessing. Job holds fast to his integrity with one hand and God's commitment to justice with the other, and he cannot let go of either or he will fall to his death. Job remains at the end the "blameless and upright" God-fearer he was in the beginning, and yet he is not the same person at all. He bears both the scars and the wisdom of his passage from then to now.

God's approval of Job's speech is contrasted with the speeches of the friends. The friends misrepresented God when they interpreted Job's suffering and, for that matter, his protests against his suffering, as God's judgment for some sin Job or his children had committed, knowingly or unknowingly. Job was right to insist on his innocence and to insist on some explanation for his condition that did not require him to abandon his integrity. He was also right that God would not welcome the kind of deceit that the friends recommended by encouraging Job to admit to some error simply to find relief, like a child admitting to doing something wrong just to get out of "time out." Job was correct to protest his innocent suffering and to resist its destructive power. He was right to seek support from his friends and to expect their understanding and loyalty in his dark, angry, and anguished days. Instead, their fear of his irreverence twisted their friendship into self-righteous condemnation.

Job was right, ironically, that God did not act in Job's case according to a retributive principle of justice, nor was Job's suffering explicable by any of the traditional justifications offered by the friends. The wicked do persist; the innocent do suffer, despite the friends' denials. Job was right. God does act with freedom—perhaps a terrible freedom at times, but also one of grace, as God's restraint of wrath against the friends demonstrates. Job was right. God has afflicted innocent persons, in the sense that the ultimate responsibility for their suffering lies with God within whose creation suffering, like joy, has a place. Finally, Job is right that God is his only source of hope and that apart from God's presence life perishes. By contrast, the friends' hope rests in the manipulation of God and, in a greater sense, with the predictability of God—a God of no surprises and nothing new. "Correct" or "truthful" is an appropriate way to speak of Job's words about God, though, admittedly, it leaves in question specific charges Job raises against God and Job's characterization of God as devious and malicious. And it still stands in tension with God's accusation, to which Job assents, that Job did not know what he was talking about.

What of the generous restitution Job receives at God's hand, however? Clearly it is not, as the friends propose, a reward for Job's repentance and supplication. Nor has Job earned it; it is not a reward for his speaking "rightly" about God. Job's possessions and family are, in the end, as they were in the beginning: a sign of God's blessing and care for Job. They come to Job by grace alone. If Job's suffering is not a sign of his guilt, neither is his wealth a sign of his innocence. The wicked may also be wealthy and the poor blessed. There is no retributive principle at work here either. The author

 Want to Know More?

About Job's wife and daughters? See Carol A. Newsom, "Job," in *The Women's Bible Commentary*, ed. Carol A. Newsom and Sharon H. Ringe (Louisville, Ky.: Westminster/John Knox Press, 1992), 131–32.

asks us to look at one instance—as he did with Job's suffering—and in this case, Job receives abundantly from God because God chooses to give to him, to return to him twice over what he had lost and more: sons and daughters, the ultimate sign of blessing in the ancient world, and another lifetime in which to enjoy them and their children's children. Job's 140 years is double the psalmist's expectation for a full, long life (see Ps. 19:10), and Job dies like one of the respected ancestors of Israel: "old and full of days." The Satan's challenge has been answered. Job worshiped God "for nothing," so God may hedge Job in protectively again, without fear that Job's loyalty is conditional.

Before the author ends his account of Job, he underscores Job's goodness one more time. God's generosity calls forth generosity from his servant, whose daughters—the only women named in the entire book—receive a portion of the inheritance, along with their brothers. Tradition called for the males to receive their portion, while daughters might become heirs only in the absence of sons. Job goes beyond what is required or expected, with an act of benevolence that testifies to his extraordinary character, recalling his self-description of his former life in chapter 29. At the end he is, in many ways, the same remarkable person we met in the beginning, and yet he has been changed forever.

What kind of ending is this? It is both fitting and disappointing. It is fitting because it affirms Job, who is innocent, honest, courageous, and tenacious throughout. It challenges the friends both about their way of befriending and their theology and narrow vision of God's justice. It affirms God's freedom—to forgive, to bless, to judge, and to condemn. On the other hand, it is a disappointing ending— a happy ending that seems to gloss over the tragic dimension of Job's experience and of human life more generally. The problem of God "doing evil," as the narrator puts it, remains. That God is responsible for Job's suffering and, by extension, for the suffering that is a tragic part of the human condition is never denied. The looming question "Why?" is never answered nor innocent suffering justified, except by the troubling implication in the whirlwind speeches that it is a part of God's design. The terrible silence of God and the experience of God's absence that so intensified Job's suffering is not justified either, and if it were a matter of divine freedom, it would seem to be a cruel choice. So much is left unanswered, and apparently intentionally so. The ending forces us to keep on asking and struggling to understand. The author of Job does not have all the answers, and neither does anyone else. The wisdom poem of chapter 28 rightly lodges such wisdom in the mind of God. Yet Job presses us to seek understanding and pushes us away from formulaic answers, theological or otherwise, and plants our hope not in answers but in a providential and surprising Creator whose praise the morning stars still sing.

We live as sufferers and celebrants, without answers to an ultimate "Why?" and for whom pain and joy and longing for God are constitutive of life. We live with chaos, asked to trust the restraining hand of our Creator and invited by Job to shout against destructive forces that diminish life or would empty it of meaning. We are people called to celebrate the creative providence of God, while embracing "things too wonderful to understand." We live with mystery, as we must, because life is always more than we can comprehend and is never satisfied with explanations. No answer satisfies our suffering "Why?" because, in truth, it is not an *explanation* we want. We want, as Job did, *God*—present in the midst of our suffering, entangled with our living. We want, as Job did, to see God and rest assured that pain and emptiness and chaos do not have the last word, that life has meaning and purpose and is governed finally by creative wisdom driven by love. Such knowledge, still too wonderful for us, invites us to live in freedom wisely and to befriend one another and the earth with tenacious love. The failure of Job's friends, after all, was not their poor advice but their lack of love and comfort. Surely it is in the face of friends and comforters and in power of their love that we see God through the tears that stain our living. Hope lives incarnate in the loving presence of another amid the doubts and fears and anguish suffering brings. Hope promises that there is more to life than evil and suffering in God's good creation. And so, as Job knows and we do too, there is.

? Questions for Reflection

1. What is your reaction to the way the book of Job ends? With what questions are you left?
2. Has Job spoken of God "what is right" in your view? Why or why not?
3. The author suggests that, though Job is restored, he is not the same person he was before. How has his "dark night of the soul" changed him? When you have passed through your own "shadows of deep darkness" (Ps. 23), how have you been changed by the experience?
4. At the end of your study, what have you learned about God, yourself, and life from the book of Job? You might try writing an ending to Job that summarizes what it means to you.

Bibliography

Brown, Robert McAfee. *The Bible Speaks to You*. Philadelphia: Westminster Press, 1955.

————. Preface to *The Trial of God*, by Elie Wiesel. New York: Schocken Books, 1995.

Clines, David J. A. *Job 1–20*. Word Biblical Commentary 17. Dallas: Word Books, 1989.

Crenshaw, James L. *Old Testament Wisdom: An Introduction*. Rev. ed. Louisville, Ky.: Westminster John Knox Press, 1998.

Guthrie, Shirley. *Christian Doctrine*. Rev. ed. Louisville, Ky.: Westminster John Knox Press, 1994.

Habel, Norman C. *The Book of Job*. Old Testament Library. Louisville, Ky.: Westminster Press, 1985.

————. "In Defense of God the Sage." Pages 21–38 in *The Voice from the Whirlwind: Interpreting the Book of Job*, edited by Leo G. Perdue and W. Clark Gilpin. Nashville: Abingdon Press, 1992.

Jamison, Kay Redfield. *Night Falls Fast: Understanding Suicide*. New York: Alfred A. Knopff, 1999.

Janzen, J. Gerald. *Job*. Interpretation. Atlanta: John Knox Press, 1985.

Murphy, Roland. *The Book of Job: A Short Reading*. New York: Paulist Press, 1999.

Newsom, Carol A. "The Book of Job: Introduction, Commentary, and Reflections." In *The New Interpreter's Bible*, 4. Nashville: Abingdon Press, 1996.

————. "Job." In *The Women's Bible Commentary*, edited by Carol A. Newsom and Sharon H. Ringe. Louisville, Ky.: Westminster/John Knox Press, 1992.

Rhodes, Arnold B. *The Mighty Acts of God*. Revised by W. Eugene March. Louisville, Ky.: Geneva Press, 2000.

Turnage, Mac N. and Anne Shaw. *Grace Keeps You Going: Spiritual Wisdom from Cancer Survivors*. Louisville, Ky.: Westminster John Knox Press, 2001.

Interpretation Bible Studies
Leader's Guide

Interpretation Bible Studies (IBS), for adults and older youth, are flexible, attractive, easy-to-use, and filled with solid information about the Bible. IBS helps Christians discover the guidance and power of the scriptures for living today. Perhaps you are leading a church school class, a midweek Bible study group, or a youth group meeting, or simply using this in your own personal study. Whatever the setting may be, we hope you find this *Leader's Guide* helpful. Since every context and group is different, this *Leader's Guide* does not presume to tell you how to structure Bible study for your situation. Instead, the *Leader's Guide* seeks to offer choices—a number of helpful suggestions for leading a successful Bible study using IBS.

> "The church that no longer hears the essential message of the Scriptures soon ceases to understand what it is for and is open to be captured by the dominant religious philosophy of the moment." —James D. Smart, *The Strange Silence of the Bible in the Church: A Study in Hermeneutics* (Philadelphia: Westminster Press, 1970), 10.

How Should I Teach IBS?

1. Explore the Format

There is a wealth of information in IBS, perhaps more than you can use in one session. In this case, more is better. IBS has been designed to give you a well-stocked buffet of content and teachable insights. Pick and choose what suits your group's needs. Perhaps you will want to split units into two or more sessions, or combine units into a single session. Perhaps you will decide to use only a portion of a unit and then move on to the next unit. *There is not a structured theme or teach-ing focus to each unit that must be followed for IBS to be used.* Rather, IBS offers the flexibility to adjust to whatever suits your context.

> "The more we bring to the Bible, the more we get from the Bible."—William Barclay, *A Beginner's Guide to the New Testament* (Louisville, Ky.: Westminster John Knox Press, 1995), vii.

A recent survey of both professional and volunteer church educators revealed that their number-one concern was that Bible study materials be teacher-friendly. IBS is indeed teacher-friendly in two important ways. First, since IBS provides abundant content and a flexible design, teachers can shape the lessons creatively, responding to the needs of the group and employing a wide variety of teaching methods. Second, those who wish more specific suggestions for planning the sessions can find them at the Westmin-ster John Knox Press Web site (**www.wjkbooks.com**). Here, you can access a study guide with teaching suggestions for each IBS unit as well as helpful quotations, selections from Bible dictionaries and encyclo-pedias, and other teaching helps.

IBS is not only teacher-friendly, it is also discussion-friendly. Given the opportunity, most adults and young people relish the chance to talk about the kind of issues raised in IBS. The secret, then, is to determine what works with your group, what will get them to talk. Several good methods for stimulating discussion are presented in this *Leader's Guide,* and once you learn your group, you can apply one of these methods and get the group discussing the Bible and its relevance in their lives.

The format of every IBS unit consists of several features:

a. Body of the Unit. This is the main content, consisting of inter-esting and informative commentary on the passage and scholarly insight into the biblical text and its significance for Christians today.

b. Sidebars. These are boxes that appear scattered throughout the body of the unit, with maps, photos, quotations, and intriguing ideas. Some sidebars can be identified quickly by a symbol, or icon, that helps the reader know what type of information can be found in that sidebar. There are icons for illustrations, key terms, pertinent quotes, and more.

c. Want to Know More? Each unit includes a "Want to Know More?" section that guides learners who wish to dig deeper and consult other resources. If your church library does not have the resources mentioned, you can look up the information in other standard Bible dictionaries, encyclopedias, and handbooks, or you can find much of this information at the Westminster John Knox Press Web site (see last page of this Guide).

d. Questions for Reflection. The unit ends with questions to help the learners think more deeply about the biblical passage and its pertinence for today. These questions are provided as examples only, and teachers are encouraged both to develop their own list of questions and to gather questions from the group. These discussion questions do not usually have specific "correct" answers. Again, the flexibility of IBS allows you to use these questions at the end of the group time, at the beginning, interspersed throughout, or not at all.

> "The trick is to make the Bible our book." — Duncan S. Ferguson, *Bible Basics: Mastering the Content of the Bible* (Louisville, Ky.: Westminster John Knox Press, 1995), 3.

2. Select a Teaching Method

Here are ten suggestions. The format of IBS allows you to choose what direction you will take as you plan to teach. Only you will know how your lesson should best be designed for your group. Some adult groups prefer the lecture method, while others prefer a high level of free-ranging discussion. Many youth groups like interaction, activity, the use of music, and the chance to talk about their own experiences and feelings. Here is a list of a few possible approaches. Let your own creativity add to the list!

a. Let's Talk about What We've Learned. In this approach, all group members are requested to read the scripture passage and the IBS unit before the group meets. Ask the group members to make notes about the main issues, concerns, and questions they see in the passage. When the group meets, these notes are collected, shared, and discussed. This method depends, of course, on the group's willingness to do some "homework."

b. What Do We Want and Need to Know? This approach begins by having the whole group read the scripture passage together. Then, drawing from your study of the IBS, you, as the teacher, write on a board or flip chart two lists:

(1) Things we should know to better understand this passage (content information related to the passage, for example, historical insights about political contexts, geographical landmarks, economic nuances, etc.), and

(2) Four or five "important issues we should talk about regarding this passage" (with implications for today— how the issues in the biblical context continue into today, for example, issues of idolatry or fear).

> "Although small groups can meet for many purposes and draw upon many different resources, the one resource which has shaped the life of the Church more than any other throughout its long history has been the Bible."—Roberta Hestenes, *Using the Bible in Groups* (Philadelphia: Westminster Press, 1983), 14.

Allow the group to add to either list, if they wish, and use the lists to lead into a time of learning, reflection, and discussion. This approach is suitable for those settings where there is little or no advanced preparation by the students.

c. Hunting and Gathering. Start the unit by having the group read the scripture passage together. Then divide the group into smaller clusters (perhaps having as few as one person), each with a different assignment. Some clusters can discuss one or more of the "Questions for Reflection." Others can look up key terms or people in a Bible dictionary or track down other biblical references found in the body of the unit. After the small clusters have had time to complete their tasks, gather the entire group again and lead them through the study material, allowing each cluster to contribute what it learned.

d. From Question Mark to Exclamation Point. This approach begins with contemporary questions and then moves to the biblical content as a response to those questions. One way to do this is for you to ask the group, at the beginning of the class, a rephrased version of one or more of the "Questions for Reflection" at the end of the study unit. For example, one of the questions at the end of the unit on Exodus 3:1–4:17 in the IBS *Exodus* volume reads,

> Moses raised four protests, or objections, to God's call. Contemporary people also raise objections to God's call. In what ways are these similar to Moses' protests? In what ways are they different?

This question assumes familiarity with the biblical passage about Moses, so the question would not work well before the group has explored the passage. However, try rephrasing this question as an opening exercise; for example:

Here is a thought experiment: Let's assume that God, who called people in the Bible to do daring and risky things, still calls people today to tasks of faith and courage. In the Bible, God called Moses from a burning bush and called Isaiah in a moment of ecstatic worship in the Temple. How do you think God's call is experienced by people today? Where do you see evidence of people saying "yes" to God's call? When people say "no" or raise an objection to God's call, what reasons do they give (to themselves, to God)?

Posing this or a similar question at the beginning will generate discussion and raise important issues, and then it can lead the group into an exploration of the biblical passage as a resource for thinking even more deeply about these questions.

e. Let's Go to the Library. From your church library, your pastor's library, or other sources, gather several good commentaries on the book of the Bible you are studying. Among the trustworthy commentaries are those in the Interpretation series (John Knox Press) and the Westminster Bible Companion series (Westminster John Knox Press). Divide your groups into smaller clusters and give one commentary to each cluster (one or more of the clusters can be given the IBS volume instead of a full-length commentary). Ask each cluster to read the biblical passage you are studying and then to read the section of the commentary that covers that passage (if your group is large, you may want to make photocopies of the commentary material with proper permission, of course). The task of each cluster is to name the two or three most important insights they discover about the biblical passage by reading and talking together about the commentary material. When you reassemble the larger group to share these insights, your group will gain not only a variety of insights about the passage but also a sense that differing views of the same text are par for the course in biblical interpretation.

f. Working Creatively Together. Begin with a creative group task, tied to the main thrust of the study. For example, if the study is on the Ten Commandments, a parable, or a psalm, have the group rewrite the Ten Commandments, the parable, or the psalm in contemporary language. If the passage is an epistle, have the group write a letter to their own congregation. Or if the study is a narrative, have the group role-play the characters in the story or write a page describing the story from the point of view of one of the characters. After completion of the task, read and discuss the biblical passage, asking for interpretations and applications from the group and tying in IBS material as it fits the flow of the discussion.

g. Singing Our Faith. Begin the session by singing (or reading) together a hymn that alludes to the biblical passage being studied (or to the theological themes in the passage). For example, if you are studying the unit from the IBS volume on Psalm 121, you can sing "I to the Hills Will Lift My Eyes," "Sing Praise to God, Who Reigns Above," or another hymn based on Psalm 121. Let the group reflect on the thoughts and feelings evoked by the hymn, then move to the biblical passage, allowing the biblical text and the IBS material to underscore, clarify, refine, and deepen the discussion stimulated by the hymn. If you are ambitious, you may ask the group to write a new hymn at the end of the study! (Many hymnals have indexes in the back or companion volumes that help the user match hymns to scripture passages or topics.)

h. Fill in the Blanks. In order to help the learners focus on the content of the biblical passage, at the beginning of the session ask each member of the group to read the biblical passage and fill out a brief questionnaire about the details of the passage (provide a copy for each learner or write the questions on the board). For example, if you are studying the unit in the IBS *Matthew* volume on Matthew 22:1–14, the questionnaire could include questions such as the following:

—In this story, Jesus compares the kingdom of heaven to what?
—List the various responses of those who were invited to the king's banquet but who did not come.
—When his invitation was rejected, how did the king feel? What did the king do?
—In the second part of the story, when the king saw a man at the banquet without a wedding garment, what did the king say? What did the man say? What did the king do?
—What is the saying found at the end of this story?

Gather the group's responses to the questions and perhaps encourage discussion. Then lead the group through the IBS material helping the learners to understand the meanings of these details and the significance of the passage for today. Feeling creative? Instead of a fill-in-the-blanks questionnaire, create a crossword puzzle from names and words in the biblical passage.

i. Get the Picture. In this approach, stimulate group discussion by incorporating a painting, photograph, or other visual object into the lesson. You can begin by having the group examine and comment on this visual or you can introduce the visual later in the lesson—it depends on the object used. If, for example, you are studying the unit Exodus 3:1–4:17 in the IBS *Exodus* volume, you may want to view Paul Koli's very colorful painting *The Burning Bush.* Two sources for this painting are *The Bible through Asian Eyes,* edited by Masao Takenaka and Ron O'Grady (National City, Calif.: Pace Publishing Co., 1991), and *Imaging the Word: An Arts and Lectionary Resource,* vol. 3, edited by Susan A. Blain (Cleveland: United Church Press, 1996).

j. Now Hear This. Especially if your class is large, you may want to use the lecture method. As the teacher, you prepare a presentation on the biblical passage, using as many resources as you have available plus your own experience, but following the content of the IBS unit as a guide. You can make the lecture even more lively by asking the learners at various points along the way to refer to the visuals and quotes found in the "sidebars." A place can be made for questions (like the ones at the end of the unit)—either at the close of the lecture or at strategic points along the way.

> "It is . . . important to call a Bible study group back to what the text being discussed actually says, especially when an individual has gotten off on some tangent." —Richard Robert Osmer, *Teaching for Faith: A Guide for Teachers of Adult Classes* (Louisville, Ky.: Westminster/John Knox Press, 1992), 71.

3. Keep These Teaching Tips in Mind

There are no surefire guarantees for a teaching success. However, the following suggestions can increase the chances for a successful study:

a. Always Know Where the Group Is Headed. Take ample time beforehand to prepare the material. Know the main points of the study, and know the destination. Be flexible, and encourage discussion, but don't lose sight of where you are headed.

b. Ask Good Questions; Don't Be Afraid of Silence. Ideally, a discussion blossoms spontaneously from the reading of the scripture. But more often than not, a discussion must be drawn from the group members by a series of well-chosen questions. After asking each question, give the group members time to answer. Let them think, and don't be threatened by a season of silence. Don't feel that every question must have an answer, and that as leader, you must supply every answer. Facilitate discussion by getting the group members to cooperate with each other. Sometimes the original question can be restated. Sometimes it is helpful to ask a follow-up question like "What makes this a hard question to answer?"

Ask questions that encourage explanatory answers. Try to avoid questions that can be answered simply "Yes" or "No." Rather than asking, "Do you think Moses was frightened by the burning bush?" ask, "What do you think Moses was feeling and experiencing as he stood before the burning bush?" If group members answer with just one word, ask a follow-up question like "Why do you think this is so?" Ask questions about their feelings and opinions, mixed within questions about facts or details. Repeat their responses or restate their response to reinforce their contributions to the group.

> "Studies of learning reveal that while people remember approximately 10% of what they hear, they remember up to 90% of what they say. Therefore, to increase the amount of learning that occurs, increase the amount of talking about the Bible which each member does." —Roberta Hestenes, *Using the Bible in Groups* (Philadelphia: Westminster Press, 1983), 17.

Most studies can generate discussion by asking open-ended questions. Depending on the group, several types of questions can work. Some groups will respond well to content questions that can be answered from reading the IBS comments or the biblical passage. Others will respond well to questions about feelings or thoughts. Still others will respond to questions that challenge them to new thoughts or that may not have exact answers. Be sensitive to the group's dynamic in choosing questions.

Some suggested questions are: What is the point of the passage? Who are the main characters? Where is the tension in the story? Why does it say (this) _____, and not (that) _____? What raises questions for you? What terms need defining? What are the new ideas? What doesn't make sense? What bothers or troubles you about this passage? What keeps you from living the truth of this passage?

c. Don't Settle for the Ordinary. There is nothing like a surprise. Think of special or unique ways to present the ideas of the study. Upset the applecart of the ordinary. Even though the passage may be familiar, look for ways to introduce suspense. Remember that a little mystery can capture the imagination. Change your routine.

Along with the element of surprise, humor can open up a discussion. Don't be afraid to laugh. A well-chosen joke or cartoon may present the central theme in a way that a lecture would have stymied.

Sometimes a passage is too familiar. No one speaks up because everyone feels that all that could be said has been said. Choose an unfamiliar translation from which to read, or if the passage is from a Gospel, compare the story across two or more Gospels and note differences. It is amazing what insights can be drawn from seeing something strange in what was thought to be familiar.

d. Feel Free to Supplement the IBS Resources with Other Material. Consult other commentaries or resources. Tie in current events with the lesson. Scour newspapers or magazines for stories that touch on the issues of the study. Sometimes the lyrics of a song, or a section of prose from a well-written novel, will be just the right seasoning for the study.

e. And Don't Forget to Check the Web. You can download a free study guide from our Web site (**www.wjkbooks.com**). Each study guide includes several possibilities for applying the teaching methods suggested above for individual IBS units.

f. Stay Close to the Biblical Text. Don't forget that the goal is to learn the Bible. Return to the text again and again. Avoid making the mistake of reading the passage only at the beginning of the study, and then wandering away to comments on top of comments from that point on. Trust in the power

> "The Bible is literature, but it is much more than literature. It is the holy book of Jews and Christians, who find there a manifestation of God's presence." —Kathleen Norris, *The Psalms* (New York: Riverhead Books, 1997), xxii.

and presence of the Holy Spirit to use the truths of the passage to work within the lives of the study participants.

What If Am Using IBS in Personal Bible Study?

If you are using IBS in your personal Bible study, you can experiment and explore a variety of ways. You may choose to read straight through the study without giving any attention to the sidebars or other features. Or you may find yourself interested in a question or unfamiliar with a key term, and you can allow the sidebars "Want to

Know More?" and "Questions for Reflection" to lead you into deeper learning on these issues. Perhaps you will want to have a few commentaries or a Bible dictionary available to pursue what interests you. As was suggested in one of the teaching methods above, you may want to begin with the questions at the end, and then read the Bible passage followed by the IBS material. Trust the IBS resources to provide good and helpful information, and then follow your interests!

Want to Know More?

About leading Bible study groups? See Roberta Hestenes, *Using the Bible in Groups* (Philadelphia: Westminster Press, 1983).

About basic Bible content? See Duncan S. Ferguson, *Bible Basics: Mastering the Content of the Bible* (Louisville, Ky.: Westminster John Knox Press, 1995); William M. Ramsay, *The Westminster Guide to the Books of the Bible* (Louisville, Ky.: Westminster John Knox Press, 1994).

About the development of the Bible? See John Barton, *How the Bible Came to Be* (Louisville, Ky.: Westminster John Knox Press, 1997).

About the meaning of difficult terms? See Donald K. McKim, *Westminster Dictionary of Theological Terms* (Louisville, Ky.: Westminster John Knox Press, 1996); Paul J. Achtemeier, *Harper's Bible Dictionary* (San Francisco: Harper & Row, 1985).

To download a free IBS study guide,

visit our Web site at

www.wjkbooks.com